PRACTI[
SOCIAL W

Series Editor: Jo Campling

BASW

Social work is at an important stage in its development. All professions must be responsive to changing social and economic conditions if they are to meet the needs of those they serve. This series focuses on sound practice and the specific contribution which social workers can make to the well-being of our society.

The British Association of Social Workers has always been conscious of its role in setting guidelines for practice and in seeking to raise professional standards. The conception of the Practical Social Work series arose from a survey of BASW members to discover where they, the practitioners in social work, felt there was the most need for new literature. The response was overwhelming and enthusiastic, and the result is a carefully planned, coherent series of books. The emphasis is firmly on practice set in a theoretical framework. The books will inform, stimulate and promote discussion, thus adding to the further development of skills and high professional standards. All the authors are practitioners and teachers of social work representing a wide variety of experience.

JO CAMPLING

A list of published titles in this series follows overleaf

PRACTICAL SOCIAL WORK

Social Work and Housing

Gill Stewart

and

John Stewart

MACMILLAN

First published 1993 by
THE MACMILLAN PRESS LTD
Houndmills, Basingstoke, Hampshire RG21 2XS
and London
Companies and representatives
throughout the world

ISBN 0–333–44666–6 hardcover
ISBN 0–333–44667–4 paperback

A catalogue record for this book
is available from the British Library.

Copy-edited and typeset by Povey–Edmondson
Okehampton and Rochdale, England

Printed in Hong Kong

Series Standing Order (Practical Social Work)

If you would like to receive future titles in this series as they are
published, you can make use of our standing order facility. To
place a standing order please contact your bookseller or, in case
of difficulty, write to us at the address below with your name and
address and the name of the series. Please state with which title
you wish to begin your standing order. (If you live outside the
UK we may not have the rights for your area, in which case we
will forward your order to the publisher concerned.)

Standing Order Service, Macmillan Distribution Ltd,
Houndmills, Basingstoke, Hampshire, RG21 2XS, England

Contents

Acknowledgements

We are grateful to Mary Brailey, Jan Owens and Moira Peelo for commenting on earlier drafts of certain chapters. Also we particularly wish to thank all those social workers whom we interviewed, for allowing us to share their insights into the housing problems faced by clients.

GILL STEWART
JOHN STEWART

1

A Social Work Approach to Housing

During the 1980s three main priorities were developed in policies for social work. 'Child protection' is now the clearer focus for work with children and families. 'Community care' is associated with the closure of long-stay hospitals and preventing the admission to residential care of elderly people and others with disabilities. Supervising 'punishment in the community' is the new emphasis for probation work. Within those policy areas, social workers engage with clients' associated housing problems, which also have their separate policy contexts. In this book we analyse the various policies and their operation in practice, and discuss ways of negotiating some resolution of the resulting conflicts.

The clients of social workers, whatever the agency – social services or probation – are almost all poor. Nearly all of them live on means-tested benefits. The majority of clients are also council tenants; if they are not, it is usually because they are without independent housing at all, rather than being home owners. Social services clients differ from probation clients on three significant demographic features. Probation clients are more likely to be male, young and single, although women, often with children, are an increasing proportion of the caseload. Given the foci of social work and given the general characteristics of the clients, problems with accommodation seem inevitable. We will be considering the extent to which social workers can become involved with the housing problems of their clients effectively, within mainstream practice.

1

First, we should take heart that work in this notoriously complex area can be effective. Social workers usually engage with housing problems at an individual level but, particularly when there is no immediate practical solution in sight, it can make more sense to work with groups of people who are similarly affected. That is why housing issues have long been a central focus for community work in this country (Lees & Mayo, 1984, ch. 6; Short, 1982, pp. 5–11), and some great housing victories have been won by local people with the support of community workers, often over a long period. Famous struggles of the past in Notting Hill, Salford, Islington and Glasgow were associated with clearance and redevelopment of an area of old private housing and the rehousing of its residents by the council (O'Malley, 1977; no comparable source on the S99 victory in Salford; Baine, 1975; Jacobs, 1976). Large scale redevelopment ended practically everywhere during the seventies. More recently, conditions in the new estates that were built under slum clearance programmes are likely to be the problem, and the council as landlord is the target for pressure (Bryant & Bryant, 1982). The situation may be different but the methods of working for change are basically the same (as elaborated in chapter 5).

Reflecting on the successful struggles of the past may encourage those already committed. But in order to counter possibly negative attitudes amongst social workers in general, we need to develop a social work approach to housing. It will be based on clients' circumstances but will avoid individualising housing difficulties that owe as much to structural and policy factors as to 'personal' problems. We begin this task by examining three analytical contexts within which housing may be understood: rights, need and problems.

Housing rights?

A place to live is a basic necessity, yet one to which we have no entitlement. There is a National Health Service in Britain, 'universal' education for children, entitlement to a subsistence income through social security benefits, but no general right to housing. There are specific rights to do with housing but these apply only to selected groups of people in particular circumstances which often reinforce rather than remedy basic inequalities. So, for example, existing council tenants have the right to buy their home – but not to rent it in the first place.

A political and pressure group campaign has been mounted for a right to rent as the prerequisite of a general right to housing, but its realisation seems a distant prospect. Supporters of a right to rent usually see it as involving entitlement of access to council housing (Labour Housing Group, 1984; Merrett, 1985). Conservative politicians have turned the idea round. A housing minister's account of 'the right to rent' during parliamentary debate sounded more like a right for private landlords to let at a profit, and this interpretation reappeared in his party's election manifesto (Conservative Party, 1987, pp. 12–13).

Free marketeers have been pressing for complete deregulation of private rented housing and public sector rents, quite the opposite of increasing rights for would-be tenants (Minford *et al.*, 1987; Ricketts, 1986). As far as the private rented sector was concerned, a housing white paper made explicit whose rights were paramount: 'laws on security of tenure . . . make it impossible to regain possession of their property [by landlords] when necessary' (DoE, 1987, para. 1.8). Following action on recommendations by the Law Commission (1987, part V) deregulation has proceeded. The Treasury characterised this aspect of housing policy thus: 'to give greater choice to those wishing to rent accommodation by enabling private landlords to make reasonable returns' (Treasury, 1989, para. 3). Evidence shows that deregulation following the 1988 Housing Act has only slightly increased lettings at the more expensive end of the private rented market, whilst confusion over rights, the harassment of poorer tenants and financial exploitation of their vulnerability and insecurity continues (Sharpe, 1991).

Whereas the Housing Act, 1980, gave council tenants the 'right to buy', the 1988 Act was promoted as giving 'most' secure local authority tenants the 'right to choose' their landlord, under Part IV *Tenant's Choice*:

[it] will change local authority tenants from dependents into consumers. Exposing local authority landlords in this way will compel them to improve the services they give their tenants if they want them to stay. Tenants will therefore benefit from a higher standard of service whether they change landlords or not. (Treasury, 1989, para. 34)

In practice it will be prospective landlords who exercise the right to choose which council properties with which sitting tenants they will buy from the local authorities. The government's version of a right to rent characterises the tenant as a consumer, assuming that the rent payer has equal bargaining power in the market place against a prospective landlord, who will be free to charge the highest possible rent. As rents are increased, and the value of Housing Benefit to assist poorer people pay the rent is eroded, so the bargaining advantage rests more securely with the landlord.

The reason why a real right to housing remains an elusive dream lies in the character of our political and social structure. Housing is regarded as property; we even use the words interchangeably. It is a major means of accumulating wealth (Jordan, 1987A, ch. 10). A Conservative election manifesto proclaimed: 'Buying their own home is the first step most people take towards building up capital to hand down to their children and grandchildren. It gives people a stake in society – something to conserve. It is the foundation stone of a capital-owning democracy' (Conservative Party, 1987, p. 11). A general right to housing would entail conflict between a substantive right of access to resources in a 'welfare state' – in this case, housing services – and the right, fundamental to liberal democracies, to own and protect property (Sampford & Galligan, 1986, discuss conflicts in rights to welfare). So an enforceable right to housing could be regarded as incompatible with a 'property-owning democracy'.

In practice this means, for example, that the legal rights of an owner to occupy or dispose of property are always likely to take precedence over a tenant's legal right to continue living in it. Tenants' protection against eviction often means little more than formally delaying the inevitable by making the owner follow due process of law in order to gain possession. This does not mean that clients' rights as tenants, or as homeless people say, are valueless – on the contrary. Throughout this book we shall be encouraging you to pursue clients' rights, for reasons of principle as well as being usually the most practical way of helping. But, in housing matters, it often seems that the scales of justice are weighted against clients and other disadvantaged people. That is what the Law Centres Federation (1986) said in their submission to the Lord Chancellor's review of how housing cases are handled in the courts: incremental administrative reform would not be enough; what we lack is housing justice.

Housing need

The absence of a general right to housing means that a selective view is commonly taken of housing issues based on perceptions of need; so we turn to the notion of *housing need* in searching for a social work approach to housing. The closest to an official definition of housing need is contained in the priorities which local housing authorities are expected to observe in selecting tenants, as listed in S22 of the Housing Act 1985: 'persons occupying insanitary or overcrowded houses, persons having large families, persons living under unsatisfactory housing conditions, and persons . . . found to be homeless'. A survey of stated allocation policies has shown that most housing authorities do broadly observe these criteria (Spicker, 1987). Councils' waiting lists are usually taken as an indication of the extent of these individual housing needs. Analysis of applicants on these lists has shown that while just under half are not immediately in need of council housing, nearly three quarters of the rest would have accepted a suitable offer of council rehousing straight away (Prescott-Clarke *et al.*, 1988, 5.1.1; and table 5.26). By the end of the 1980s inner city local authorities were, mainly, housing only people for whom they accepted a statutory responsibility because they were homeless. Across all housing authorities, a third of new tenants in 1989–90 were homeless households (DoE, 1991A, fig. 69, p. 89). The traditional waiting list notion of need has become less relevant.

Some of the waiting list criteria may be irrelevant but they are not unreasonable, for in the early eighties, 800 000 households were statutorily overcrowded (OPCS, 1986, table 5.30). By the mid-1980s 2 868 000 dwellings were still in poor condition, of which half a million lacked one or more basic amenities, such as a toilet or a sink (DoE, 1988). And by the end of the decade 145 000 households per annum were formally recognised as homeless, two and a half times the number in 1977 when the specific legislation was passed (DoE quarterly homelessness statistics). The mention in the 1985 Act of 'large families' tends not to mean much in practice, except to emphasise the general priority given to families with children in public housing policy. However, these figures alone demonstrate that officially defined housing needs are a long way from being met, and a closer look at the definitions shows the criteria themselves to be inadequate and restrictive.

Definitions of 'insanitary' conditions are inherited from 1930s public health legislation and concentrate on plumbing. The usual standard for measuring overcrowding is 1.5 people per room not counting the kitchen, with complex rules about which household members can be allowed to share a bedroom. Children under ten are counted as half a person, and babies not at all. The result can be particularly hard on lone parents who are expected to share their bedroom with younger children. The popularity and rapid growth in owner occupation has meant that people with low incomes are now involved, often buying houses in poor condition: half the unfit houses in the country are owner occupied. However both homeowners and existing council tenants tend to be regarded as adequately housed by definition which, for the latter, may preclude even a transfer.

The clearest example of restrictive criteria concealing the extent of housing need is found in the homelessness legislation. The law defines being homeless as: 'having no accommodation which the applicant and those of his family with whom it is normal or reasonable for him to reside, is entitled to occupy.'[1] But then it goes on to specify 'priority need groups' who qualify for help. Homeless people deemed not to be in 'priority need' are excluded from rehousing rights and also from being counted in the homelessness returns. The effect of this is that single homeless people and couples without children, who are those least likely to receive priority, are officially invisible. The detail of homelessness legislation is complex and we deal with what social workers need to know in practice at appropriate stages later in the book. The purpose here is to make a point about restrictive criteria of housing need.

In response to these serious shortcomings in traditional methods of describing housing need, the Greater London Council initiated an extensive survey, carried out by the London Research Centre, of people living in London to discover what really were their requirements. It found that there were a quarter of a million 'potential' households in London consisting of people who were reluctantly sharing, usually with relatives, and did not have a place of their own (London Research Centre, 1988, section 3; for background see Pawson & Tuckley, 1986, and Rauta, 1986); 69 000 of these potential households described themselves as 'trapped' in their present sharing arrangement due to lack of money or inability to obtain council housing. While the London survey gives a realistic picture of how many poorer people are actually living, the discovery of unmet housing need on such a scale is not politically popular.

Right wing economists (Minford *et al.*, 1987, p. 118) were knocking at an open door in calling for council tenants to be restricted to 'renters of last resort' whom they characterised as the poor, the old, the handicapped and the unfortunate; for, under Thatcher governments, the policy emphasis moved steadily towards providing only for people with these 'special needs', everyone else being expected to make their own arrangements in the private sector. The proportion of public sector dwellings completed each year which were 'special needs housing' increased during the eighties from a fifth to a third of a declining number of completions – just 13 000 in all for 1989–90 (DoE, 1991A, fig. 69, p. 89). This policy has some appeal for social workers, because it seems to give priority to elderly and disabled clients and to people leaving mental hospitals, and to recognise their particular difficulties in obtaining decent housing.

But the promotion of 'special needs housing' can be criticised on three grounds. First, from a practice viewpoint it can be stigmatising; 'special' implies not 'normal', and this may be both undesirable and unacceptable to clients. Sheltered housing for old people may encourage dependency (Butler *et al.*, 1983). Secondly, separate specialist housing provision has the effect of setting the priority of one group of people in serious housing need against another group in equally serious, but different, housing need. The groups are seen to be in competition for the specialist housing which exists. Thirdly, and more generally, concentration on 'special needs' is argued to be strategically unsound. The implication that only the residual problems of a particularly vulnerable minority require official attention encourages complacency and provides the government with a justification for not having a general policy for housing at all.

The housing problem

In order to focus attention on the housing policies of government and away from individuals and their perceived needs and deficiencies, a leading housing policy analyst (Malpass, 1986, ch.1) recommends that we concentrate on the nature of 'the housing problem', which he defines as being to do with quantity, quality and access. It is not a new approach, though no less useful for that: Engels wrote in similar terms in 1872 about 'the housing question'.

The country's housing stock is notionally divided into four sectors reflecting its ownership: owner occupied; public rented mainly from a local authority; private rented from an individual landlord or company; and a voluntary sector including non-profit making and charitable organisations, mainly housing associations. About a third of households in England and Wales (substantially more in Scotland and Northern Ireland) are tenants, renting their home from a landlord; most of those are council tenants. In Britain as a whole, over two thirds of households own the house or flat which they occupy though only a minority are outright owners, with 59 per cent repaying a loan, usually a building society mortgage (CSO, 1987, p. 137; OPCS, 1986, from table 5.13).

A simple polarisation between an unsubsidised owner-occupied sector and a subsidised public rented sector can no longer be sustained. The government's role has been dominant: 'The Government welcomes the growth of owner-occupation, which it has strongly encouraged . . . helped by mortgage interest tax relief' (DoE, 1987, paras 1.7–8). The cost to the Treasury of giving tax relief on mortgage interest payments was estimated at £4 750 million in 1987–8 though the government does not regard this as public expenditure (Treasury, 1988, pp. 112–13). By contrast, the capital expenditure on housing which the government recognised, in the public sector, stood at £2155 million in 1989–90; a two-thirds decline since the start of the decade (DoE, 1991A, table 64, p. 81; Malpass, 1990, pp. 20–1). In justification the government has stated with conviction that:

> clearly, the majority of people wish to own their own homes. This wish should in the Government's view be supported. Home ownership gives people independence; it gives them a sense of greater personal responsibility; and it helps to spread the Nation's wealth more widely. These are important factors in the creation of a more stable and prosperous society, and they justify the favourable tax treatment accorded to borrowing for house purchase by owner-occupiers (DoE, 1987, para. 1.7).

Quantity

In housing literature the term 'need' usually means '. . . need to build dwellings', hence it can be a synonym for 'quantity' as used here, rather than differentiating the *housing* from other needs of individual applicants for a council home.

Although home ownership has increased from a third of the housing stock in the 1950s to two-thirds by the late 1980s, this does not represent a real increase in the quantity of housing available. The increase in owner-occupation has been a long-term trend at the expense of the rented sectors. Privately rented housing has declined from 90 per cent of the stock after the first world war, mainly being demolished under slum clearance programmes and replaced by new council building and, more recently, through sale for owner occupation.

The sale of council houses under the Housing Act 1980 at discounts to tenants of up to 70 per cent has greatly added to owner occupation. Formerly public rented houses have become owner-occupied houses by a paper transaction, and without their occupants moving. The change constitutes a loss of stock to the public sector and to present and future generations of people who must rent because they cannot afford to purchase. As a modest counter-action to such criticism, which will release council tenancies for re-letting, the government is also encouraging 'cash incentives' to help tenants buy privately (DoE, 1991A, para. 7.21). But with a million sales by September 1986, 15 per cent of public sector rented housing had been lost in six years of 'the right to buy' (CSO, 1987, p. 137, table 8.16, and DoE quarterly housing statistics).

Current government public house building policy allows local housing authorities which are able to sell the most houses also to build the most. It is the popular suburban and rural areas with traditional houses which have the greatest scope for new building because of high sales, rather than the areas of greatest housing need. The inner city authorities, particularly in London, have been severely constrained over new building because relatively few tenants have exercised their right to buy (National Audit Office, 1989, para. 3.8). On the other hand, those suburban and rural local housing authorities where sales are high argue that housing need is often greater in such areas than it is in northern metropolitan towns and cities. Their association has estimated that overall suburban and rural authorities need to build 162 000 dwellings (Bramley & Paice, 1987). To meet these estimated needs, housebuilding – 83 per cent of which was private – has been around 179 000 annually (DoE, 1991A, from fig. 67, p. 85).

Quality

While the quantity of available housing has declined overall, the general quality of the stock has not been improving in a uniform manner. A survey of English local authorities found that 84 per cent of housing in the public sector in 1985 required, but was unlikely to receive, on average nearly £5000 worth of renovation work per dwelling (DoE, 1985A, p. 5). The situation is worse in Scotland with dampness a chronic problem (House of Commons Scottish Affairs Committee, 1984). Repair and improvement of older houses in the public sector is complicated by the low quality of industrialised dwellings built during the 1960s and 1970s, which require major work after little more than a decade of use (we discuss conditions on these rundown modern estates in chapter 5). The government has complacently claimed that 'the local authority stock is generally in a sound condition and that there has been no deterioration during the previous five years' whilst local authority improvements and conversions have risen steadily from 84 700 in 1984 to 160 000 in 1989 (Treasury, 1989, para. 25 and table 9.10).

Disrepair should not be regarded as the problem of just one sector. By 1986, 52 per cent of the houses in poor condition were in the owner-occupied sector: this represented about one in twenty owner-occupied houses, an increase of more than a third in 14 years (DoE, 1988; DoE 1982). As more dwellings come into owner occupation by various routes, this sector's proportion of the unfit dwellings could be expected to increase on statistical grounds alone. More significant are the growing numbers of old people in the poorest quality owner-occupied housing, and a chronic persistence of the highest proportion of unfit housing in the private rented sector. Even the Conservative-controlled Association of District Councils acknowledges that there has been little improvement in the standard of housing since 1981, with 1 in 7 still in poor condition at the end of the 1980s and grants not being channelled to the areas of greatest need, in the north of England (Association of District Councils, 1989). Financial help available via local authority grants for repair and improvement of privately owned housing fluctuated during the eighties, depending on 'targeted' schemes (for instance, roof repair), and declined to a level of 111 000 grants per annum after 1986 (Treasury, 1989, table 9.17). Legislation was introduced which would further 'target' the help on people with low income by way of means-tested grants – this is discussed in chapter 6.

Access

Although the main determinants of access to commodities in a market economy are clearly wealth and scarcity, there may be structural barriers operated by institutions which systematically exclude particular groups. The barriers which impede access to housing vary between the tenures, and vary with the differing objectives and powers of those institutions controlling access to each tenure. The critical barrier to owner occupation is income, operated by the controlling financial institutions of building societies, banks, and insurance companies, but often mediated through estate agents and solicitors in a way which does exclude, or channel into less desirable properties, certain groups of people.

In the next major tenure, public renting, allocating tenancies is not motivated by the desire to maximise profits. The barriers to access in this case are the interpretation by local government officers, within a legal framework, of 'housing need' criteria. Such criteria tend to invert commercial concerns, hence people who are 'worse off' in housing terms, and probably therefore poorer, should have priority over other applicants. Private landlords just like the institutions of owner occupation, are driven by the profit incentive. However, other motives, such as managing tenancies and regaining possession of them, introduce complexities into straightforward financial dealings. The combination of profit motive and easy vacant possession are a powerful consideration in letting private property. If it would be more profitable to use the residential property for another purpose, the landlord must be able to gain vacant possession. It therefore makes commercial sense to discriminate in favour of those groups whom one can evict more easily when allocating private tenancies, within the confines of law of course.

Some structural barriers to access occur across the tenures, although manifested in different ways within each. The exercise of institutional racism is one such barrier. Black minorities are known to be relatively disadvantaged in the quality of their housing (Brown, 1985) and local studies show how this happens in relation to specific sectors.[2] West Indian and Asian people have more difficulty than white applicants in obtaining an offer of a council tenancy, and tend to be concentrated in the worst housing and/or on less desirable estates. This was a consequence of working practices in the housing departments concerned; added to which were the attitudes and racially harassing behaviour of white tenants.

Turning to the private sectors, it has been found that black prospective house purchasers in inner cities were considerably less likely than white buyers to get a building society mortgage. They were expected instead to make private arrangements or to seek commercial loans at higher rates of interest, often on the advice of an estate agent or solicitor (Karn *et al.*, 1985). In Rochdale, building societies operated rules whereby they would not lend on houses without front gardens, under a certain price, or located in certain areas of the town. These rules had the indirect effect of discriminating against Asian applicants for mortgages (Commission for Racial Equality, 1985B).

Non-white and ethnic minority households are under-represented among private tenants in London, where numbers living in private rented housing are twice the national average. Ethnic minority tenants reported greater difficulty in obtaining private rented accommodation, higher rents, worse conditions, less security and more harassment than white tenants (Pawson, 1986, pp. 21–2). Despite the law, because of the way in which one seeks a private tenancy, private landlords are able to exercise open discrimination between would-be tenants. A recent study confirmed widespread discrimination by landlords and has shown that accommodation agencies will usually collude with landlords' preferences, or discriminate directly themselves (Commission for Racial Equality, 1990). In that study, landlord discrimination was found to be at its worst in cities or areas of cities with high ethnic minority concentrations. The practical effect of accommodation agency discrimination is that people from particular minority groups will tend to be directed to landlords who belong to the same minority – Hindu, Irish, Jamaican – thus increasing concentrations in poorer areas of the city.

Another kind of impediment to access is discrimination on grounds of household composition. We have already mentioned the general preference given to families with children in public sector allocation policies and that its effect is to restrict access for people who live in other types of household, particularly single adults of working age. While single people form three in ten of the working population in England and Wales, they comprise only 7 per cent of council tenants (Venn, 1985). Access through homelessness procedures is even more restricted, with only 5 per cent of households accepted by local authorities being 'vulnerable' single people of working age. People without children fare better with housing associations and co-operatives, maybe because of the voluntary sector's concentration on 'special needs' housing. Only about a quarter of new housing association tenants are families with children while about two fifths are adults of working age, mostly living alone.[3] However, housing associations control only 2.2 per cent of the stock (CSO, 1987, p. 137).

Having a job with earned income is usually a prerequisite for obtaining a mortgage. Having been denied access to the other sectors, for one reason or another, single, unemployed and particularly young people congregate in what private rented housing remains available. A government survey found that 58 per cent of recent private renters were under 30 and a high proportion were unmarried. Most of them shared rooms and facilities with other 'tenants'. These young adults were in what is termed 'non-exclusive use occupancy licences' and more often than not the landlord was resident. A fifth of these new renters had moved straight from their parental home (Todd, 1986, paras 4.1, 4.2 and 6.6). Many clients of the probation service are in this situation.

Our analysis of the nature of 'the housing problem', has provided an essential policy context for the rest of the book. But housing policy analysis is necessarily about government, organisations, finance and buildings rather than about people; and social work practice concerns people. So it is time to move from a 'macro' level of discussion about policies and take a more 'micro' analytical approach to people's housing problems. Social workers have to start with clients' circumstances and the need to respond to them individually, within their family networks or in local communities. It may be difficult to remember the policy contexts and structural constraints that surround particular problems, but it is important to maintain that balance.

Clients' housing problems

Increasingly, during the eighties, people turned to advice agencies for help with housing problems. There is no more of an obligation on local authority housing departments to give personal help with housing problems than there is on the DSS to advise about welfare rights; so people in difficulty turn elsewhere. As an indication of the scale, housing was third only to social security and debt as the subject of enquiries made to citizens advice bureaux throughout the country in the middle of the decade. Housing and social security problems, often inter-related, together topped the list in London CAB (NACAB, 1986, p. 3; Childs *et al.*, 1985, p. 14).

There has been very little recognition of the demands made on social workers by people with housing problems. For instance, a major study of advice-giving in London identified all kinds of potential helpers including GPs, but made no mention of social services departments, the youth service or probation (Borrie, 1982). Lack of focused research means that it is hard to find firm evidence about the incidence and nature of housing problems among the clients of social work agencies.

Probation

The National Association of Probation Officers (NAPO) has estimated that 'about half of all probation service clients live in lodging, bedsits, hostels or some other form of temporary accommodation' (NAPO, 1985). The traditional image of an offender with accommodation problems has been of a middle-aged man with no fixed address and under voluntary after-care on release from prison, and there still are many men in this situation among the regular clientele of inner city teams. A comprehensive survey of inmates of penal institutions in the south-east found that 30 per cent had been homeless when they offended and many more could expect to be so on release (Banks, 1978; also Fairhead, 1981).

However another wide-ranging study of probation case-loads in South Yorkshire showed that the typical client seeking help with accommodation was aged under 25 and on a statutory supervision order (Hine *et al.*, 1976, p. 5). More recent experience of the impact of DSS board and lodging benefit regulations confirmed that this was still the case, and highlighted the urgency of housing problems among younger clients (Stewart *et al.*, 1986b). A cautionary tale about the importance of taking housing seriously can be read between the lines of the report on the IMPACT experiment in the early seventies that tried, but apparently failed, to reduce reconviction rates through 'intensive situational treatment' in small caseloads. A third of the probationers concerned were living in hostels or lodgings or were literally homeless, but in only 9 per cent of cases did the probation officer give any special help with finding better accommodation. The response to financial difficulties was similar and perhaps reflected a wish to avoid the welfare image associated with giving 'material aid', although the clients rated these material problems very seriously (Folkard *et al.*, 1976, pp. 5–6, 8). This alone does not account for the outcome of the whole IMPACT experiment, but neither can it have helped.

Housing now has a higher profile in the probation service, with development officers appointed in several areas to pursue ordinary housing possibilities, rather than only hostels and lodgings. NAPO's commitment is evidenced by their establishing a housing working party and publishing an information pack for members, with an exhortation: 'We confidently assert that the provision of decent housing generates [positive] attitudes and that it is important to develop such opportunities for clients' (NAPO, 1985, p. 1).

Social services

Social services departments are bigger organisations than probation areas, with more practitioners (including non-social workers) and more clients in varied circumstances. So, it is not surprising that locating evidence about the incidence of clients' housing problems is difficult, particularly as this is not a statutory area of work for social services. Caseload monitoring studies have shown what the client's main problem is considered to be at an early stage of contact with the agency – at referral, intake or case allocation. If only one presenting problem was recorded, it involved housing in about 15 per cent of cases; when several different problems were recorded for each client the proportion related to housing rose to around 25 per cent. The incidence of recorded housing problems is fairly consistently within this range, showing only limited increase from the mid-seventies to the mid-eighties and in a diversity of areas with varied tenure distributions, for example: Croyden, Dereham (Norfolk), Lancashire, North Yorkshire, Plymouth, Selly Oak (Birmingham), Southampton, Strathclyde and an unidentified Welsh town. The main points from these studies will be raised below.

Housing problems seem to be closely related to recorded levels of financial problems, although these are considerably higher among families with children, less so for older clients. Sometimes housing and money have been aggregated as 'material' problems (for example, Balloch *et al.*, 1985, for the Association of Metropolitan Authorities). In reality, disrepair and dampness combined with fuel debts, rent or mortgage arrears and consequent fear of eviction can cause feelings of crisis and despondency for the people concerned. When clients' views are sought, they say that housing is what worries them more than anything; help from social workers is particularly appreciated. For their part, social workers find housing problems among the most difficult to handle; possibly because the solutions are so obvious yet so hard to achieve (Glampson and Goldberg, 1976; Sainsbury *et al.*, 1982, pp. 44–6, 67; Sinclair & Walker, 1985, pp. 51–3, 65; Stevenson & Parsloe, 1978, pp. 36, 322, 370).

Clients with unresolved housing problems expressed the most dissatisfaction as consumers of social work in an area team in Sheffield and a GP health centre in south London (Sainsbury *et al.*, 1982, p. 46; Corney, 1981, p. 169). It is probably true to say that people who are regarded as having only 'material' problems receive less attention than any other group in social services departments. An intake team in Birmingham adopted an explicit policy of not dealing with callers who brought only housing or welfare rights queries (Black *et al.*, 1983, pp. 135, 182–4). To protect themselves from bombardment, that team of social workers had made an open policy out of what most teams probably do tacitly in practice.

Contrary to casework mythology, whereby social workers are thought always to reinterpret a presenting practical difficulty and invest it with deep psychological meaning, all the evidence is that hard-pressed practitioners will take the client's request at face value and rarely probe further. From Southampton in 1975 to Glasgow in 1985, about 90 per cent of clients with presenting housing problems received some perfunctory information or advice and the case was closed within a week, usually the same day (Goldberg & Warburton, 1979, pp. 73, 86–7; Becker & Macpherson, 1986, p. 42). Numerous other local studies during the intervening decade showed the same systematic screening-out process at work. Most of these clients were self-referred. They had actively sought help by taking themselves to the social services departments rather than being sent there by another agency such as the court or a hospital. The social workers' apparent lack of response and effectiveness in such circumstances represents a lost opportunity for genuinely preventative social work.

There could scarcely be a greater contrast with long-term family caseloads. In two small-scale qualitative studies of social work with the parents of children living at home under supervision, practically all of them were said to have raised housing difficulties with their social worker during the period of contact. Similarly, social workers in three agencies in Sheffield reported that 88 per cent of their clients had discussed housing problems with them in the course of a year (Thoburn, 1980, pp. 33–5; Mattinson & Sinclair, 1979, p. 33; Sainsbury *et al.*, 1982, p. 16). On this evidence, it seems that a much higher proportion of social services clients have current or potential housing problems than are recognised at the initial referral stage.

One possible explanation could be that social workers' attitudes to their clients' difficulties mellow over time. They may start with assumptions about acceptable levels of dissatisfaction with living conditions which clients are expected to tolerate, then become more responsive as a helping relationship progresses. For example, in one town where an unusually low incidence of housing problems was reported, the researchers commented: 'Provided that families were not too choosy about where they were housed, housing was not a difficulty in Normanton (Wakefield), and only a small proportion of referrals raised the need for accommodation for people who were living temporarily with relatives and/or were overcrowded' (Hadley & McGrath, 1984, p. 97). This somewhat restricted definition of housing difficulty would have discounted anyone living in bad conditions, an attitude which social workers would have found hard to maintain over a long period of contact with a client.

The authors of another study reporting a particularly low level of housing problems in Wandsworth, an inner London borough with high housing stress, suggested that the answer to any discrepancy lay in problem perception:

a client's problem status is not a purely personal attribute in the same sense, for example, as their age. A client is or is not 47 years old, but if she is a battered wife she may be regarded as having a housing problem, a marital problem, a financial, a personality problem, or any combination of these and other problems. How she is labelled will depend, in part, on the views of those with whom she comes into contact. (Sinclair & Walker, 1985, p. 64).

Social workers' initial view of clients is partly determined by the circumstance of referral. Referral from an official agency under a statutory provision, like a supervision order from the juvenile court, can imply that controlling a child's behaviour is what is required, whereas the mother of the same child might present herself as having a housing problem which is causing domestic stress. As a result, the same family's circumstances are perceived differently (Sainsbury *et al.*, 1982, p. 11, discuss this).

Ill-assorted lists of what are thought to constitute housing problems are given in these local social services studies: disrepair, dampness, lack of facilities, overcrowding, insecurity, homelessness, lack of furniture, moving house (Goldberg & Warburton, 1979, p. 146; Becker & Macpherson, 1986, p. 29). Reminiscent of the housing policy approach which we discussed earlier, this list is less useful for analysis of practice. It includes situations of both greater and lesser seriousness and which are qualitatively different; situations where rehousing is required as well as those where the existing housing can be improved, or the difficulty resolved by relatively small expenditure of money. Most importantly, the list does not readily relate to clients' circumstances in social work terms. There is no reason why social workers should be expected to help everyone in these situations. We need to know what else is going on in people's lives that makes it appropriate for them to be clients of a social work agency, rather than just a housing advice agency. Otherwise the question is raised whether they would be better off going elsewhere. Perhaps social workers are justified in screening-out callers with only 'material' problems.

The quantitative method used in caseload monitoring has the effect of separating-out one aspect of clients' circumstances and isolating 'material' problems from the rest, presumably developmental or relationship problems. This reinforces the criticisms of those who argue that helping clients with housing problems is not 'real' social work (for example, Stevenson & Parsloe, 1978, p. 199). It is our contention that social workers' ability to help clients *is already* seriously diminished by ignoring their material circumstances. The substantive issue is one of boundaries and competence. Clarification in this area is reason enough for our writing a book on *social work and housing*, to try to encourage more confident and effective practice.

Understanding and responding to clients' circumstances

If social workers are to be helpful on housing matters they must first identify the problem, then – with the client – work out what can be done about it. This includes not only responding to difficulties which clients raise, but also means looking for background housing issues which may not be mentioned if the client has taken them for granted as an unchanging part of life. To do this means learning to 'think housing' about every case and understand the housing dimension of each client's circumstances.

For intervention to be effective it must be appropriately focused, so you have to understand the nature of the client's housing problems or where the difficulty is located. For instance, it is not useful to concentrate on trying to get someone who is living in bad conditions rehoused if there is little chance of success and the existing accommodation could be improved to an acceptable standard. When the facilities, or state of repair, of the housing itself, are the problem then it – or the landlord responsible for keeping it in that state – should be the focus for change. Of course, this is unlikely to be straightforward or the client could probably have handled it themselves.

There is more to housing problems than leaking roofs and faulty plumbing, serious though these may be. The house is where people spend most of their lives, usually in close proximity to other people. It can be of an objectively adequate standard as a building but have ceased to meet the needs of some or all of the people living in it. Change in relationships between members of a household can make it difficult for them to tolerate each other's company. The wellbeing, independence and even personal safety of individuals may be endangered by their having to continue living together under the same roof. At least one person has to move for this situation to be resolved, usually the weaker party.

Sometimes people's unsatisfactory circumstances are said to be the result of their own limitations. Some clients are thought to be incapable of maintaining a home or of managing in independent housing. Others allegedly choose to live in chaos or to lead a 'rootless' lifestyle. To this way of thinking, individuals' problems are self-inflicted, so appropriate solutions are tolerance, permanent support or control; help to improve their housing is considered to be irrelevant. But that attitude itself can be reinterpreted as representing the real problem. Societal reaction to particularly marginalised groups of people leaves them ostracised as deviant. When social workers also subscribe to this view, their clients' rejection is compounded. Similarly, disablist attitudes among professionals and service planners can restrict housing opportunities for clients with learning difficulties, for example, paternalistically and in their 'best interests'. Trying to counteract the labelling process and offer positive help to people who have been damaged by institutionalisation, or stigmatised because of where they live – in a lodging house or on a difficult-to-let estate – can be a real challenge to social workers.

A typology of housing problems and plan of the book

From the above basis of locating where the problem lies, we can construct a typology which is useful for analysing clients' circumstances and social work responses in practice. The order of the following typology reflects both the significance of the associated housing problems within social work and, for practical purposes, the order of chapters in this book. The first type of problem arises from breakdown or other change in relationships between members of the household. In type two, the problem may seem to be with the individual but this should be seen in the context of societal reaction to particular groups of clients. The third type of housing problem lies in the standard of the housing itself or the conditions under which it is occupied. It is often aggravated by the client's deteriorating health.

This typology of housing problems will be used as the framework for the rest of the book. Chapters 2, 3 and 4 each develop in a different way type one in our typology of housing need. We start with parent–child relationships and that most common rite of passage, leaving home. In chapter 3 we look at different aspects of relationship change and breakdown between adult partners, often in circumstances of violence and threats. Following directly from relationship breakdown comes consideration of family homelessness in chapter 4. In chapter 5 we develop type two and the social worker's role with clients who are disadvantaged and stigmatised because of where they live: those who used to be called 'problem families' housed on difficult-to-let estates. Chapter 6 is about the housing itself as the problem, type three, and we concentrate on helping older people to continue living independently in their own homes.

Of course the 'types' of housing problem are not entirely discrete and they sometimes overlap – both in reality and within the chapters of this book. Thus housing conditions are a major source of difficulty on the estates described in chapter 5, but differently from the circumstances discussed in chapter 6. 'Difficult' estates are not amenable to piecmeal improvement but, most importantly, their residents tend to be regarded as a class apart from the rest of society, with consequent implications for their rights of citizenship. And homeless families are equally stigmatised while they live in temporary accommodation, as are young single homeless people, although in either case homelessness may have arisen from breakdown in a relationship with partner or parents. As with most typologies, what we propose is not a rigid categorisation but rather a heuristic device for understanding the issues. Consideration of housing *solutions* in social work – the various forms of supported accommodation and special schemes for access to 'ordinary' housing, which are the mainstay of 'care in the community' – is both outside the focus on housing *problems* and beyond the limited capacity of this book.

In order to keep the discussion firmly rooted in practice and related to clients' circumstances, we often use illustrative case examples. Most of these come from research which we have conducted in various social services departments and probation areas, in particular, a local study of clients with accommodation problems in the north of England and interviews with social workers who work with homeless people.

Essential aspects of a social work approach to housing include starting where the client is, and not isolating the housing problems from what else is going on in people's lives. So, for example, we deal with money problems and benefit issues as they impinge on clients' housing situations, as they often do. Most clients are poor: over two-thirds rely on means-tested benefits and social services, clients alone make up between a fifth and a quarter of all income support claimants (Stewart & Stewart, 1986, p. 1; Becker & Macpherson, 1986). Many more clients are tenants than owner occupiers, as shown in the local social services studies we discussed earlier (for example, Sainsbury *et al.*, 1982, p. 10), and three-quarters of council tenants receive housing benefit to pay at least a part of their rent (CIPFA, 1986, pp. 5–6), so most clients are likely to be receiving housing benefit.

A difficulty often experienced by social workers and, of course, clients is the veiled antipathy which exists between many housing advisers and welfare rights workers. This is probably to do with perceptions of the expertise involved in each other's tasks and their respective ability to achieve what counts as a solution. The effect is that housing advisers tend not to know about the range of social security benefits and welfare rights officers cannot advise about housing rights. Social workers need to know about both, at least enough to be able to ask appropriate questions and find out the answers. So money matters are covered when they arise in relevant contexts and details of the most useful housing and welfare rights guides are given together in the Resource List.

Avoiding the complex and ever changing technical detail of benefit regulations, we concentrate instead on key contextual points and general strategies. The same goes for treatment of homelessness legislation, tenants' rights and assistance with repairs or improvement – to give three housing examples where technical detail is important and liable to change. Helping with clients' housing problems is, in many respects, a very practical matter; so practitioners need to become familiar with the relevant tools for this trade – such as the national rights guides and local information sources – and to learn what arguments work in which situations.

But there are no standard formulae for practice. Any book which tried to tell practitioners, in detail, 'how-to-do-it' would not only become out of date before it was published, but would also risk misleading social workers who must ultimately rely on their own skills, experience and initiative when advising clients and negotiating with other agencies. The most appropriate and achievable objectives for academics who write books intended for practitioners are: first, to alert the reader to the dimensions of an issue; prompting relevant questions to ask, and where to seek answers. Secondly, to suggest criteria for formulating strategies towards some kind of solution, and for dealing with possible failure, whilst acknowledging that tackling some problems is beyond the competence of basic grade practitioners – social workers cannot do everything. Thirdly, building practitioners' confidence on the basis of information about what others have been able to achieve in similar situations. In this context the presentation and discussion of relevant social work research can enable practitioners to feel informed, and it provides evidence to support them in dealing with their own management and other agencies. Academics are expected to mediate research findings and make them accessible to a practitioner and student readership.

Central to a practice agenda for social work and housing in the 1990s must be the basic and enduring values of respect for persons, particularly the current emphasis on anti-discriminatory practice; and client self-determination, entailing work in partnership *with* clients rather than *on* or *for* them. Because people with housing problems often appear to be the victims of powerful bureaucracies – the DSS and its front line, the Benefits Agency, as well as Homeless Persons Units, Housing Benefit Sections and other parts of local authority and voluntary sector housing organisations – advocacy becomes an essential skill. Housing problems are not quickly resolved and tend to recur, so encouraging clients' self-advocacy can be particularly valuable, enabling them to work the system or at least to survive its depredations. Real empowerment of someone in the vulnerable position of a homeless applicant may seem rather ambitious, and is scarcely within the gift of an ordinary social worker; but group work with powerless people can enable them to generate mutual support and to benefit from each other's experience.

Social workers are considered to be 'professional' as opposed to 'citizen' advocates; but when confronted with the implacable determination of a housing official or the technical wizardry of a welfare rights officer, many social workers may feel almost as powerless and de-skilled as their clients. However, for those who have the stamina, lobbying local policy makers and service managers, either direct or through active membership of BASW, NAPO or a pressure group, can be a constructive method of system intervention. Campaigning is a form of self-advocacy for social workers.

Notes

1. S58(1),(2) of Part III of the Housing Act 1985, which supersedes and consolidates the Housing (Homeless Persons) Act 1977.
2. The local studies are to be found in: Simpson, 1982; Commission for Racial Equality, 1984; Commission for Racial Equality, 1985A; Phillips, 1986; Commission for Racial Equality, 1986; Henderson & Karn, 1987.
3. For the sources see Underwood *et al.*, 1986, p. 14; Ramsay & Smith, 1987, table 2, p. 8; Hales & Shaw, 1990, ch. 3 in which children as an element in household composition are omitted; and McCafferty & Riley, 1989, ch. 4 – on co-operatives – in which a quarter of households have children and two-thirds were economically active.

2

Moving to Independence: Leaving Home, Leaving Institutions

Leaving the parental home is normal; most of us do it sooner or later, usually in adolescence or young adulthood. But it can be a protracted and difficult process. Leaving home is not only a matter of finding somewhere else to live, although that can be hard enough. It also entails a loosening or severing of family relationships and the assumption of a more autonomous lifestyle. Following the typology which was outlined at the end of chapter 1, one theme running through this chapter will be parent/child relationships between adults: the changing dependent and caring roles between generations in families, and how tension in these relationships interacts with difficulties in access to alternative housing. A second theme will be the meaning of independence and how this is presented as a main objective in current social policies.

Clients of social work agencies do not represent a norm in the population as, more or less by definition, they are people with problems. Where leaving home is concerned, some of these problems are caused by restrictions on practical options which are also shared by a much wider group of people. So we start by looking at the constraints experienced by ordinary young people in general as a context for understanding the more complex circumstances of people who become clients. Then we consider the position of those whose move towards independence is indirect, via a period in care or custody, and

27

the services which are intended for both young and older single homeless people. Independent housing is central to the government's policy of 'care *in* the community' for people leaving mental hospitals, while 'care *by* the community' can entail 'children' continuing to live with their parents beyond youth and remaining dependent on them because of disability or learning difficulties. Finally, dependency roles may be reversed with adult 'children' (sons and daughters) caring for their parents in old age. Led by government policies, social workers increasingly set up 'independence' as the goal which clients are expected to attain; but we need to consider how desirable and realistic this is in practice.

Policy contexts

Government housing, social security and employment policies form the practical context for young people leaving home and may be a major source of constraint upon them. The dependency of pensioners on state benefits and services is structured by both social policies and normative expectations, and links between poverty and disability are similarly entrenched in the benefit system. Women who care for old and disabled people are generally dependent either on men or on the special 'invalid care allowance' which is set at a level below basic income support, so they have to claim means-tested benefits in order to rise above the poverty line (Glendinning, 1990). The financial dependence of people on low rates of benefit and on each other can trap them in dependent relationships when they might prefer to be free.

Structured dependency of young people on their parents is a complex phenomenon which recent governments have cultivated as a matter of policy in the inter-related areas of housing, money and work. Social security and employment policies are age-related and predicated on young people living with their parents, which presents an automatic problem of how to pay for independent accommodation on leaving home (we have discussed this elsewhere, Stewart & Stewart, 1988, as have others, for example, Roll, 1990).

People under 25 comprise more than a third of the registered unemployed, and a series of policies during the latter half of the 1980s contrived to make their position much worse. First they were subject to special regulations which required them to move on from lodgings after a short period or take a drastic cut in benefit, then the abolition of board and lodging regulations effectively closed that housing option altogether. Those under 21 were removed from the protection of Wages Councils on the grounds that they had priced themselves out of work. Those under 25 were allowed an age-related benefit rate 22 per cent below that of their elders because, it was argued by ministers, they were not fully independent and should be living with their parents. Then people under 18 were disqualified from benefit in their own right altogether. The only permitted alternative living with parents or a job to was on the Youth Training Scheme (irrespective of whether a training place was actually available), thereby fulfilling a Conservative election manifesto pledge that youth unemployment would become a 'thing of the past'. All of these measures have undermined poorer young people's ability to become self-reliant. While temporary exemption from benefit disqualification is possible on grounds of 'severe hardship', usually requiring validation by a social worker or another authority figure, the money allowed is insufficient to pay for even the lowest – standard accommodation.

Surveys of young people's housing preferences have shown conventional aspirations; most want to live independently and to own their own homes, but relatively few expect to do so while they are still young. A survey conducted for the Department of Education's Review Group on the Youth Service (1983, p. 23) found that three-quarters of those asked expected to have difficulty in obtaining accommodation on leaving home, but nevertheless to have left before they were 25; half thought they would leave home in their teens. Local studies in Scotland, Bristol, South Wales and Kent found predictable class and gender differences: girls tend to leave home at an earlier age than boys and young men are more likely to return to their mothers when problems arise; young people from working-class backgrounds experience most difficulty with finding work and accommodation and managing on a low income, and this prospect deters many from leaving when they would otherwise wish to. Young people from middle-class backgrounds are less likely than others to move for negative reasons, associated with family tension, and report the least difficulties overall (the main studies are reviewed by Furlong & Cooney, 1990).

Low wages and high unemployment among young people make it unlikely that more than a few can afford to buy their own homes. Meanwhile, council house allocation priorities discriminate indirectly against the young unless they have children of their own, as we explained in chapter 1. Even where there is no formal age barrier to single people registering on an 'active' waiting list, a young person will have to wait longer to accumulate enough points for rehousing than someone older who has already lived in the area for many years. Points are usually attached to length of local residence as well as to housing need criteria. The historic concentration on building family-sized housing, in all sectors, means that there are relatively few small, one-person dwellings and these go mainly to old people. Any local authority will give priority to a pensioner's application for a one-bedroomed flat in preference to a teenager who wants to leave home. Some inner city authorities – including Glasgow, Liverpool, Manchester and Newcastle – have developed schemes for allocating housing which is 'difficult to let' to single people, including the young. These tend to be flats in high rise blocks, which are not considered suitable for families, and on unpopular estates such as those described in chapter 5.

Housing policies which give priority to families with children have led some commentators to suggest that young women deliberately become pregnant in order to obtain a council flat. There is no systematic evidence for this and it seems more likely to be a rational explanation for what happened, offered by some young mothers after the event. This interpretation is supported by Griffin's (1985) analysis of girls' attitudes to motherhood. Clark (1989) found that teenage mothers were shocked at the suggestion of anyone using a baby to obtain a council flat, and other researchers have reported worsening housing problems rather than any solution after the birth of a first child (for example, Phoenix, 1991). Sharpe's (1987) account of interviews with teenage mothers who had ended up living in poverty and isolation, in the worst housing their local authority could offer, would act as a deterrent to any girl seriously contemplating pregnancy as a passport to prosperity.

Young people who are allocated a council flat usually take it, despite all the problems, because independent housing is so hard to obtain and it can be the only way out of a tense domestic situation. Others less fortunate have to rely on the rapidly diminishing private rented sector, traditionally the habitat of 'transient' youth. While only about 10 per cent of the population nationally rent from private landlords, 40 per cent of household heads under the age of 25 year old heads of household do so (*Social Trends* 16, 1986).

By the mid-eighties, the majority of new private lettings in most areas were insecure, unprotected and expensive, particularly shared board and lodging arrangements (Stewart *et al.*, 1986). Around 52 000 unemployed young people lived in board and lodging accommodation before restrictive benefit changes in 1989. A survey by the Social Security Policy Inspectorate reported that 40 per cent of them had moved in after a 'dispute' with parents or relatives, and another survey of the residents of 'houses in multiple occupation' (HMOs) in Scotland found young people who had left their parents' home made up a fifth of boarders from all age groups (DHSS, 1986, p. 9; Currie & Miller, 1987, pp. 40–1).

In the face of these difficulties in obtaining access to independent housing, it is not surprising that many young people who are unmarried stay at home, or soon return to their parents after a period away on their own. The Census (analysed by Venn, 1985, p. 9) shows that half of all single people of any age live with their parents or grandparents. In parts of east London, and no doubt elsewhere, one in four households are like this, containing another 'potential household' unable to leave (Pawson & Tuckley, 1986). The National Child Development Study (discussed by Jones, 1987) confirmed that the general Census finding applied to young people but it did not represent a fixed state: two-thirds of men and over four-fifths of women had already left home at least once by the age of 23, and about half of them went back again.

Working with young people and their parents

Many youth workers spend much of their time advising young people who are trying to leave home about housing options and the limitations to what is available locally. The dilemma is to try and give constructive advice without encouraging false hope and a rash move. Tyler (1978, pp. 33–5) describes the early involvement of youth counselling services while Wiggans (1982) gives a detailed account of work with young people leaving home in north-western industrial towns. He identifies the important supportive role which youth club workers can have with potentially homeless young people who live 'away from the bright lights' and are not in contact with any more formal agency.

Workers from two different youth agencies in Greater Manchester have contributed particularly useful and sensitive accounts of the pressures involved in detached and club-based work with young people who are leaving home. They demonstrate a need for what is effectively a specialist area of youth work, yet one which is in demand in most local agencies, to be better recognised by management and strengthened by mutual support networks among workers (Masterson, 1982; Cox & Cox, 1977). Young people leaving home became a pressure group cause in the late eighties and numerous resource packs and training manuals were produced for local and national use.[1] Such publications can be an asset for the inexperienced worker and save duplication of effort.

But as Masterson (1982) stresses, young people leaving home need to be accepted and listened to as much as they need practical advice, which they may not eventually pursue. Psychotherapists Haley (1980) and Kraemer (1982) suggest strategies for working with disturbed young people who are in the process of leaving home. However, as these are based on family therapy, with its assumptions about the organic integrity of nuclear family living, they will be unpalatable to some social workers and may be inappropriate for helping young people who have become the family scapegoat. Young people on the brink of independence expect to be treated as individuals.

While unemployed young people are unlikely to approach conventional social work agencies, they may come to the notice of local authority social workers who are involved with the family in another capacity, perhaps working with younger children or with the parents in their own right. In the following case, the mother is the client. She had first been referred to the area team for child care reasons eight years previously, as a homeless family. At the time she was living in the top flat of a 26-floor high rise block with her two sons aged 21 and 16; another daughter had already married and moved away. The problem was:

> the family situation. Client would now like to be independent of the two boys but there is a care order on the second son and she is named as responsible parent with whom he resides. Client would like smaller living unit on her own but cannot fulfil the local authority's conditions for accepting transfer applications ie. the property must be decorated to a certain standard. She could manage her money but sons exploit her and do not cooperate in better budgeting. Difficult to effect any change in present family climate and dynamics. Could be resolved satisfactorily for client if the two sons moved out.

What can the woman's social worker do? It is not in the sons' financial interests to leave home and finding alternative accommodation would be difficult; they would probably have to move into board and lodging. The co-operation of the 16-year-old's social worker could be sought to persuade him to make a financial contribution to the household, which would entail getting income from a training scheme place. Alternatively, there might be a supported lodgings scheme run by the authority for teenagers in care, which would enable him to move out. The mother, as tenant, could apply for a transfer without her elder son who would not have security of tenure in his own right. A volunteer decorating scheme could solve the problem of the housing department's condition for transfer. Such a scheme might be run by the probation service, using clients on community service orders, or by the local council of voluntary service using Employment Training labour (ironically). An example set by the younger son could put pressure on the 21-year-old to behave more considerately towards his mother.

In this case it seems that the two sons would not leave home because they thought they were better-off where they were. More often, the young person wants to move but cannot see a way of doing so, as with an unemployed 24-year-old man living with his parents in an owner-occupied suburb. He was described as suffering from reactive depression.

> Client in dispute with parents, spends most of his time in his room, needs and wants own accommodation. Needs to become independent of mother. Client has contacted housing associations and housing department to no avail. Will not look at hostel type accommodation due to stigma attached.

Realistically, access to decent-standard private rented accommodation is barred to unemployed young people without enough capital for a deposit. Perhaps the parents could be persuaded to come up with some rent money as the price of restoring reasonable relations with their son when he left home. But the mother may not want to let go of her son. Staying in the social services department's mental health 'independence unit' might be more acceptable to the client if it were clearly understood to be temporary. His chances of getting a permanent tenancy would be greatly increased by moving in there first, as a quota nomination scheme had been negotiated for residents with a local housing association. The diagnosis of reactive depression suggests that a move away from home was the only solution, but a transitional period in supported accommodation could be helpful to prevent isolation and continuing depression.

Young people living alone in bedsitters are found to be generally more lonely, depressed and insecure than their peers in other kinds of accommodation (Francis, 1982A, pp.

106–8). On the other hand, people who do not leave home and continue living with their parents after their mid-twenties, are more likely to lack personal confidence and to become increasingly isolated and defensive in their personal relationships (Francis, 1982B, pp. 127–9). This can mean that their motivation to become independent declines along with anyone else's ability to help. McRae's study of long term unemployed young people found that a fifth, mostly girls, had internalised their position and blamed themselves for their lack of work (in White (ed.), 1987). Young women who have been unemployed for a number of years and who are still living with their parents are probably most vulnerable. A 28-year-old woman lived with her parents in their owner-occupied home in a village. Her GP referred her to a psychiatric social worker because she was wetting the bed, usually a stress reaction:

> There is friction between client and mother, mainly due to the fact that they are under each other's feet all the time. Consequently client may benefit from having a place of her own. Accommodation not seen as a major problem by client. Unwilling to look at alternatives due to her financial position. Would be in a much better position if she was employed.

A social worker faced with this situation might have to consider confronting the relationship between mother and daughter before tackling the primary need to leave home. Such intervention might well be unacceptable to the client and her mother, and most social workers would probably give up trying.

Leaving care

Every year around 14 000 young people aged between 16 and 19 leave local authority care – this is less than one per cent of the age group as a whole, but they feature disproportionately in surveys of homeless people and among the inmates of penal and psychiatric institutions with nowhere to go on discharge (relevant research will be discussed below). Care leavers are affected by housing, social security and employment policies and they share similar constraints with their contemporaries who have not been in care. However they are often seriously handicapped by their childhood experiences and disadvantaged by their position as 'children of the state'.

Young people who leave care in their late teens will commonly have been admitted from unstable and destructive family circumstances whose effects can be long lasting. The issues are illustrated by a residential social worker's description of a 16-year-old boy who had been received into care when he was five and ended up in a secure unit:

> The boy is removed from the problem areas – his family and the neighbourhood where they live. He cannot adjust to these settings [the secure unit] effectively while in security. Being in care offers him safety and warmth that is not available at home. It is hoped that the cycle of solvent abuse, absconding and petty theft will be broken and the boy can be reintroduced to his family. The family are severely disabled – father is blind, mother severely mentally ill. It is hoped the boy will be able, through successful leave, to return and live at home.

For that young man, and many others, there is little prospect of returning home when the time comes to leave care, because the problems which led to admission have not been resolved. Meanwhile he reacted to his distressing situation by harming himself and antagonising others, and the care system's response was over-protection. Nevertheless he must leave care and fend for himself at an arbitrary age – in a year's time – much younger than other young people who have been relatively undamaged by their childhood. His family are in no position to support him, either emotionally or financially, and as an unqualified, working-class boy he will be at the mercy of the state's most punitive social policies. A social worker's most positive contribution in these circumstances could be to encourage self-advocacy, enabling the client to identify and express his own needs, with some expectation that the care authority would listen rather than pursuing a standard policy of rehabilitation to the parental home.

Understanding support from a residential social worker could increase the likelihood of the boy's wishes for his future being taken seriously.

Pressure groups, politicians and researchers became interested in the subject of leaving care during the 1980s, after a long period of neglect. The main qualitative study by Stein and Carey (1986) also summarised the findings of others. Principally they questioned the appropriateness of independence as the goal which care leavers are expected to achieve and the value of independence training, which was likened to a 'domestic combat course' that young people must pass as a condition of being offered housing. As most of the care leavers who were interviewed by the researchers wanted to live with other people, not alone, social skills which would be required for inter-dependence were suggested as being more useful. Inability to seek help and support was often a major problem for young people who had learned not to trust adults, were used to being told what to do, and had been taught that they must achieve self-reliance. When given independent housing they were likely to abandon the tenancy rather than seek help with debt management or to counter the loneliness which accompanies independence. Yet at the point of leaving care, most of the young people concerned had accepted that independence was their goal; they had absorbed society's expectations.

These research findings suggest that the most useful contribution by ordinary social workers could be facilitating mutual aid groups among prospective care leavers, so that they have a support network to fall back on in the future (also recommended in Department of Health guidance, 1991B, para. 9.22). The Children Act 1989 places a duty on social services departments and other care providers to prepare young people for leaving care, and on local social services authorities to provide accommodation and 'advice and assistance' thereafter up to age 21. Compared with previous policies under the Child Care Act 1980, which imposed no duties and the upper age limit for discretionary help was lower, this is a major improvement. However the new Children Act remains primarily an enabling measure insofar as care leavers are concerned. Most of its provisions are still in the form of discretionary powers, rather than enforceable duties, which are qualified by imprecise or unhelpful definitions. In any case the available funding is considered inadequate for implementation.

To illustrate these points, young people must be defined into a category of 'children in need' whose welfare is likely to be 'seriously prejudiced' without accommodation; and they may be offered a bed in a community home as 'accommodation', however inappropriately. Social services departments generally have no housing resources of their own, and ability to fund voluntary organisations which offer this service may just mean more financial security for the agencies concerned, not necessarily any increase in provision. A duty on housing departments to co-operate applies only if it 'does not unduly prejudice the discharge of any of their functions' (discussed further in chapter 4).

Care leavers as such have no priority under homelessness legislation and although the Code of Guidance for housing authorities recommends that they should look favourably on young people 'at risk', this is dependent on goodwill in local policies.[2] Surveys (for example, by Bonnerjea, 1990; Abrahams & Mungall, 1989) have shown inconsistency in the level and nature of local authorities' provision for care leavers, which is likely to continue so long as discretion and underfunding prevail. In these circumstances, the acknowledged 'possibility that the implementation of the 1989 Act might result in young people being sent to and fro between departments or authorities', seems inevitable (DoE *et al.*, 1991B, p. 21).

Despite these misgivings there is much positive potential in the leaving care provisions of the Children Act 1989 and the accompanying revisions to the homelessness Code of Guidance. It is up to practitioners and managers to make what they can of the positive spirit in the new policies, despite undoubted shortcomings in their resourcing and statutory force. The practice guidance issued from the Department of Health is, in most respects, constructive and realistic; many points are evidently based on practice feedback and on the research findings which have been mentioned above (DoH, 1991B, ch. 9).

The essential components of preparation for leaving care are said to be (para. 9.45):

Enabling young people to build and maintain relationships with others (both general and sexual relationships);
Enabling young people to develop their self-esteem;
Teaching practical and financial skills and knowledge.

The methods which are recommended are practical, responsive to consumer opinion, and sensitive to equal opportunities issues, particularly concerning race, disability and sexual orientation (less so on gender). The desirability of taking risks is emphasised, backed-up with a responsibility to deal with failure.

The housing needs of care leavers are clearly recognised but there is inadequate guidance on how to persuade housing departments to fulfil their half of the duty to co-operate. Acknowledging that 'the priority afforded to providing housing for young people leaving care is a matter for consideration locally', the DoH 'strongly encourages' social services departments to: 'liaise with housing associations, who may prove receptive to the needs of those young people leaving care who are not judged to be a priority for council housing' (para. 9.82). Reliance on the voluntary sector may be, realistically, the best solution but one for which SSDs would have to pay: the social services authority, rather than any housing source of funding, would be expected to grant aid voluntary projects – putting care leavers in competition with other groups for resources under the Children Act.

The DoH guidance is non-committal about the organisation of aftercare services, except to say that whoever has been 'most closely involved' with a young person whilst in care should remain in contact thereafter (para. 9.64). But the experience of leaving care teams suggests that this is not necessarily desirable. Young people of this age may prefer to make a break with their past and will not always welcome the continuing intervention of a childhood authority figure. It is essential that aftercare should be in a form which is acceptable to potential clients, so there may be advantages in a specialist team of workers who can concentrate on the needs of care leavers alone. Stein and Carey's research (1986) found that some young people had rejected help at the time of leaving care then regretted it later on.

Leaving custody

Most probation clients under statutory supervision are young, as annual statistics from the Home Office show: over a third come into the narrow 'young offenders' age bracket 17–20 years. This makes social policies which affect young people leaving home especially relevant to probation work. Survey evidence indicates that probation clients are much more likely than those of other agencies to be without independent housing and therefore dependent on formally provided services or informal support from relatives (Stewart & Stewart, 1991, pp.17–18). Another finding, which may help to explain this situation, is that around half have spent at least part of their childhood in care, so cannot necessarily rely on the family back-up which most young people leaving home would expect (evidence cited in Stewart *et al.*, 1989, para. 5.22).

It appears that for young offenders problems with access to housing and lack of money are closely inter-related and both are commonly associated with conflict in the family and release from custody. The Code of Guidance on homelessness mentions young offenders leaving custody as an example of young people 'at risk', along with care leavers, and in some respects the two groups are interchangeable: many young people in practice leave care via a period in custody. Despite these considerations, it is commonly assumed that young offenders will live with their parents on release from custody. A national survey conducted by one of us found that two-thirds of people under 17 in custody were expected to return home, with little indication of how realistic this was. The destination for most of the rest was unknown, and special placements in supported accommodation were being arranged for only 2 per cent (Stewart & Tutt, 1987, p. 142).

The direction of criminal justice policy for the 1990s is towards 'punishment in the community' as the alternative to custody, for all but the most serious young offenders, and the probation service is to be responsible. The close supervision which it is intended that probation officers will exercise over offenders requires that they take an interest in housing, because it would be difficult to maintain surveillance over someone who is homeless (acknowledged by the Home Office, 1988, para. 3.18).

Homelessness has been traditionally associated with voluntary after-care for discharged prisoners and as such was marginalised from the mainstream of probation work. 'NFA', meaning a person of no fixed abode, represents a powerful negative stereotype for probation officers (as Rojek *et al.*, 1988, argue). Home Office research (for example, by Fairhead, 1981) confirmed that homelessness was commonplace among those older single men who were likely to become voluntary after-care clients after serving short prison sentences; but the characterisation of this group as 'persistent petty offenders' did nothing to encourage positive attitudes towards working with them. Instead, any attempt at resettling 'NFAs' was commonly left to unqualified and lower paid ancillary workers, whose failure would serve to reinforce the stereotype of an unhelpable client group (as in a project researched by Corden & Clifton, 1985). Effective work with marginalised clients requires greater, not less, skill and experience than average.

In the mid-1980s there were signs of a wider awareness within the probation service of the varied nature of clients' housing problems; this included a willingness to think in terms of housing, as applicable to everyone, rather than 'accommodation', which was something different, provided only for clients. The National Association of Probation Officers (NAPO) issued a resource pack on *Probation and Housing* to its members. Nearly all of the After-Care Units changed their names to, for example, Probation Housing Unit, and broadened their clientele accordingly. The Home Office instructed areas to develop Area Accommodation Strategies which would cater for a range of local needs (circular 35/1988). Practitioners in many areas became involved in community development initiatives on local difficult housing estates and were encouraged in this by the Home Office's *Statement of National*

Objectives and Priorities (1984, para. 3; Henderson, 1986; Hope & Shaw, 1988).

That new enlightenment may, however, have been short-lived. The Home Office's white and green papers which set the agenda for the 1990s envisaged that the resettlement aspects of after-care, and anything to do with housing, would be removed from probation officers' sphere of work and contracted out to the voluntary and private sectors, on the grounds that: 'Arranging for, and actually providing, accommodation for offenders are both functions which require expertise distinct from professional probation skills'. This policy change was supported by political arguments, familiar from social services community care policy, which promoted the 'independent' sector for its own sake and in pursuit of that elusive goal, 'value for money', which is assumed to be attainable only through 'the disciplines of the market' (Home Office, 1990, paras 9.13, 10.5, 10.9, 10.16).

Two decades of an increasingly 'coercive tilt' in Home Office policy for the probation service have demonstrated probation officers' resilience in pursuing client-centred practice, in the face of contrary pressures. But the material pressures on clients have worsened at the same time as social policies have constrained probation workers' ability to help. Benefit changes are thought by practitioners to have seriously threatened the viability of resettlement work with homeless offenders. Initial success in applying for Social Fund grants was compromised by the need to collaborate with DSS officials, thereby stigmatising clients. Subsequent restrictions have made it increasingly difficult to furnish tenancies and even to obtain deposits and advance rent, while the abolition of boarders' benefit has jeopardised the continuing existence of supported lodging schemes, which were the main local resource for probation teams in many areas (Fowler, 1987; Nottingham, 1989). It is important that main grade probation officers should give continuing priority to tackling clients' housing and financial problems, and be supported in this by service management. Otherwise the expectation of confronting 'offending behaviour' becomes unrealistic when taken out of context of the offender's social circumstances.

Leaving hospital

Resettling the patients discharged from long-stay hospitals has been regarded as a social work task ever since community care became the stated objective of health and welfare policies in the early 1960s. The NHS and Community Care Act 1990 makes it a responsibility but the practicalities of achieving independence for this institutionalised group remain far from clear in the Act and its voluminous accompanying guidance.

The importance of adequate housing has frequently been stressed in policy documents, for example in the white paper which preceded the 1990 Act: 'The Government believes that housing is a vital component of community care and it is often the key to independent living' (DoH *et al.*, 1989, para. 3.5.1). Social services departments must consult housing departments (and housing associations) when making their Community Care Plans, with the objective of providing a 'seamless service for users'. But both departments are told to 'determine their objectives and priorities within the resources available' and warned that, 'care management systems will have to operate in the context of these decisions' (DoH, 1990, paras 1.2, 3.6). Separate draft guidance to housing authorities makes it clear that they will receive no extra funding and that they are not, in practice, expected to do anything more: 'There is no change in long-standing policy . . . the impact should be gradual. These developments in community care policy do not fundamentally alter the role of local housing authorities, or the priorities to be observed in catering for their various types of clients' (DoE, 1991C, para. 4).

The confusion continues in sections of the guidance which are addressed to practitioners, rather than planners. They are informed that: 'Care management is based on a needs-led approach . . . [to] assessment of the user's circumstances in the round', which appears to be positive support for good practice, although it is recognised that 'assessment does not take place in a vacuum', but tends to reflect the availability of services. There is a requirement to, 'bring apparent housing . . . needs to the attention of the appropriate authority and invite them to assist in the assessment', but no consequent duty to provide housing nor even, apparently, to respond at all in individual cases. The existence of unmet needs has to be fed back into the planning process where they can compete in the setting of future priorities (DoH, 1990, pp. 23–9).

Experience of collaboration between housing and social services, over what could be described as community care, has varied according to the tier of government and other characteristics of the authorities concerned, and especially with the client group. For older people and others with physical disabilities, it is usually a matter of improving or adapting existing housing in order to keep the person living independently in their own home and accommodate any carer: this is in support of the government's policy for 'care *by* the community' (as we discuss in chapter 6). Negotiations have generally been concerned with the allocation of sheltered housing if care needs could be met only through a move. A survey of ten local authorities in the early 1980s suggested that co-operation in this area was reasonably good, although dependent on local goodwill in the absence of standardised procedures (Hearnden, 1984).

The picture is different when we consider the position of people with learning difficulties and particularly those who have been diagnosed as mentally ill. At issue is the provision of 'care *in* the community', in the form of housing and support services, for people leaving mental hospitals. The needs of the majority who are already outside institutions have scarcely been considered. Department of Health statistics showed a 28 per cent decline in both in-patient populations over a decade and that three times more alternative residential places were provided for former mental handicap hospital patients, although the number of psychiatric hospital beds closed was nearly double. People who have been hospitalised for mental illness are unlikely to receive continuing 'care in the community', and it seems that in most cases no one knows what happens to them (as shown in local surveys, for example, by Kay & Legg, 1986).

Research into the attitudes and practices of housing workers identifies 'care in the community' as a recurring area of conflict with social workers. The Audit Commission (1989A, para. 84) reported that: 'Every housing department visited had experienced difficulties over referrals from social services and health authorities, particularly over the discharge of ex-psychiatric patients under care in the community policies'. Such applicants were often considered to be '"unrehouseable" – that is, unable to sustain an orthodox council tenancy without guaranteed social work support . . . because they have a duty to help the most vulnerable, [housing staff] are being forced into an area where their skills and resources are inappropriate' (Niner, 1989, p. 78).

One solution would be for Homeless Persons Units to reject applications from the 'vulnerable' groups: thus DoE statistics show that only 3 per cent of acceptances for rehousing during 1990 were on grounds of mental illness. Another common reaction is to expect social workers to undertake assessments in 'problematic' areas, which half of all housing authorities did 'as a matter of course in the case of mental illness or handicap', leaving their staff feeling 'generally relieved' (Evans & Duncan, 1988, p. 29; Niner, 1989, p. 32). Perhaps in recognition of these attitudes, and as a trade-off, inviting housing departments to co-operate under the new legislation, the DoH guidance advises social services departments that they 'should recognise that the assessment process they originate may be used by other agencies to assist them in fulfilling their statutory responsibilities, for example by local housing authorities in assessing homelessness applications' (DoH, 1990, para. 3.3). How housing departments use social work assessments may be another matter. In practice they often seem to be discounted as, for example, in the legal test case on 'vulnerability' involving Waveney District Council's rejection of a homeless man called Bowers (1982 3 All ER, pp. 727–32). This is frustrating for social workers but the alternative, of not co-operating with housing staff, can mean even less housing opportunity for discharged patients. Arms length co-operation, following procedural ground rules agreed by management, probably offers the best prospect. In single tier authorities social services representatives can usefully remind housing officers of their council's corporate responsibility for homelessness.

The emphasis throughout the 1990 Act is on local authorities as purchasers rather than providers of community care.

They have an obligation to promote the 'independent' sector, comprising private and voluntary organisations. The relevant national charities are ambivalent about the future prospects for local authority housing while keen to promote their own role (for example, Wertheimer, 1988 & 1989). Central government subsidies for 'special needs' housing provided by voluntary housing associations has already increased the possibilities for some of the people discharged from mental hospitals (a review of the various forms of supported accommodation and schemes for access to 'ordinary' housing would be beyond the scope of this book). Voluntary projects running group homes, for example, commonly have management committees composed of local professionals; and social workers can usefully serve on these committees. In return for not a lot of time spent supporting project staff they are able to exercise an element of quality control over how the scheme is run, and can ensure access for their team's clients.

Accommodating discharged mental hospital patients may be the only subject on which the DoH guidance makes an apparently categorical statement: 'Patients who have lost their homes should not be expected to leave hospital until suitable accommodation has been arranged'. This is to avoid placing 'even greater burdens on particular services . . . where a person becomes homeless as a result of leaving inappropriate accommodation which has been provided following discharge from hospital' (DoH, 1990, paras 3.25, 3.44). Whether this can be achieved with no projected expansion in housing provision will remain uncertain until after the Act's implementation in 1993. But it is a positive statement of principle, suggesting a clear role for social workers as advocates who might be able to turn the rhetoric into reality.

The evidence indicates that those discharged patients, for whom no suitable and acceptable accommodation has been arranged, tend to move between a state of homelessness and makeshift arrangements with relatives. As we noted with young offenders leaving custody, social workers and hospital staff usually assume that patients who were admitted from a family home will return there and increasingly, as hospitals reduce their admissions, relatives are expected to care for people with learning difficulties and those in mental distress.

This situation can impose stress on carers and cared for alike. It has long been recognised that psychiatric breakdown may be associated with tension and enforced dependency within the family (the evidence is reviewed by Perring *et al.*, 1990). On the other hand parents who continue caring for their adult 'children' into old age face dilemmas and anxiety when the time comes for the dependent person to move away from home (Richardson & Ritchie, 1989).

Without increased resources, it seems unlikely that social workers can offer much help to such families; their prospects for well-being are limited by the practical options available. Unfortunately the Jay report's principled declaration, that adults with learning difficulties should have the right to leave their parental homes, was not followed by a sufficient expansion in services (Jay, 1979, para. 133). So what can practitioners do? At least they must not lose sight of the principle. They should try to facilitate self-advocacy in both clients and their carers and discuss the options openly, avoiding collusion with the sexist basis of policies which expect women to provide care indefinitely.

The single homeless

Homelessness has been a recurrent theme throughout this chapter, because it is a common experience among people leaving institutions. The phrase 'single homeless' is used as shorthand for single adults and couples without children who are literally homeless and sleeping rough, or who use the circuit of hostels, night shelters and other forms of houses in multiple occupation (HMOs) which can be found in most towns and cities and which claim to provide for the 'single homeless'.[3] It is thus a circular definition and an arbitrary one, insofar as it includes couples, who are not single, while excluding lone parents, who are. This categorisation reflects the long-standing emphasis on families in British housing policy and the over-riding priority given under homeless persons legislation to households which include children (discussed in chapters 1 and 4).

However the concept of 'single homelessness' long pre-dates contemporary housing policies: it has been traced back to Tudor times and originates in its present form from the nineteenth century. The group attracts a high degree of social stigma arising from fear of deviance from settled, familial conformity, and this is expressed in the use of perjorative language: in academic literature as well as in fiction and the popular press, single homeless people are often referred to as vagrants, tramps, drifters, destitutes, dossers, down-and-outs (Archard, 1979; Cook, 1979). They have traditionally been a focus of activity for organised Christian religion of all denominations and, for example, the Salvation Army remains probably the largest single provider of hostel accommodation, although at the beginning of the 1990s that position is under review (Moore *et al.*, 1991; Logan, 1989; Sorensen, 1986).

Whether overtly religious or not, the great majority of agencies catering for the single homeless are run by voluntary organisations and over the decades this has been an area noted for inter-charity politics. Dissension has focused mainly on how the client group is perceived and presented: under a medical model, emphasising individual problems and support needs; or following a structural analysis which concentrates on policy change for improved access to ordinary housing. Social workers and probation officers who are concerned with the single homeless need to understand these issues if they are to work effectively with the voluntary organisations which are the main service providers; but they should resist taking sides in charity politics unless substantive questions of good practice are at stake. Over-identification with one organisation may antagonise others, to clients' disadvantage.

The staff in these voluntary organisations often work long hours under difficult conditions, living with demanding residents, for very low pay. They may feel put-upon by workers from statutory agencies, whom they see as dumping clients on them without a proper explanation. It is unfair to refer clients with particularly challenging behaviour to volunteer settings which lack the requisite expertise. On the other hand the staff in voluntary hostels and night shelters are likely to welcome the interest shown by statutory workers who take the trouble to visit their establishment and find out how it works. This also enables you to give an informed account to clients, or at least to know as much about the place as they already do. It is perhaps the least consideration a client should expect before they are 'referred' to a 'placement' where they may have to live for the foreseeable future.

Research methods employed on the subject of single homelessness have been mainly quantitative, the preoccupation being to measure the population and identify its characteristics. Large-scale surveys commissioned by central government have found it to be a heterogeneous group with ordinary features and primarily housing needs (Drake *et al.*, 1981). Others seeking, for example, 'to obtain information on the mental health of London's destitute', have highlighted psychiatric problems among single homeless people (Weller *et al.*, 1989; and for example Whynes, 1990). Young homeless people (defined variously as under 18, 21 or 26) have been considered separately and their cause has been championed, as an aspect of child protection, by the national children's charities with nineteenth century religious origins, such as Barnardo's and the Children's Society. Academic research about homeless young people has concentrated on the agencies which have been set up to help them (for example, Brandon *et al.*, 1980; Liddiard & Hutson, 1991) and it has largely been left to those agencies to publicise the needs of their clientele, with assistance from the mass media (Brynin, 1987).

Latterly a major concern of central government research funders was to identify and cost the 'care' provided in hostels for single homeless people. This research was in support of the DSS's policy of transferring responsibility for 'care', as opposed to 'hotel', costs to local authority social services departments under the NHS and Community Care Act 1990 (Berthoud & Casey, 1988; Garside *et al.*, 1990). Since the mid-1970s, social workers have been involved in resettling hostel residents, particularly under hostel closure and upgrading programmes undertaken by inner city housing authorities such as Glasgow, Liverpool, Manchester and the London boroughs of Camden, Lambeth and Westminster. Usually the social workers have been employed in specialist teams by social services departments, but also by health authorities or voluntary organisations which have been set up for the purpose, and some housing departments employ resettlement staff with social work experience (the range of hostel resettlement projects is reviewed by Dant & Deacon, 1989; Coleman *et al.*, 1990, discuss shared training issues, but not from a specifically social work viewpoint).

As with homeless families (chapter 4), very little has been written about social work with single homeless people. The few specialists who have written about their work stress its mainstream nature and the marginality of the client group. The latter's needs and capacity for change are thought to be similar to those of other adult client groups, but isolation and experience of rejection makes many single homeless people reluctant to accept social work help (chapters by Salton and McCanney in Stewart & Stewart, 1982; Fellows, 1979; Morfett & Pidgeon, 1991; Breton, 1991). The single homeless were not even mentioned in a book about *Social Work with Undervalued Groups*, so marginalised are both the client group and social work with them (Wilkes, 1981).

Cultural relativism may be partly responsible for that neglect. The lifestyle of the open road has been romanticised and the principle of self-determination may be cited to support non-intervention with clients who are thought to have chosen a way of life or to be incapable of accepting anything better. This approach ignores the lack of effective choice which is generally available to homeless people. A preference for the least restrictive alternative should not be confused with positive choice: for example, the only affordable housing which is available may entail an unacceptable level of supervision.

Much of resettlement social work is concerned with trying to improve clients' access to basic services which the rest of us take for granted, health care being the main example. Difficulty in registering with a GP leads to over-use of hospital casualty departments, where single homeless people are treated badly. Following recognition of the problem by the Royal Commission on the NHS, special health care projects for the homeless were set up, mainly in London. But critics, including some of the medical staff involved, have concluded that separate provision merely institutionalises neglect by the mainstream service which continues unaffected (Merrison, 1979, ch. 7; Jeffrey, 1979; Williams & Allen, 1989).[4]

Professional attitudes to single homeless people were not necessarily improved by pressure group campaigning to stress their normality and housing need. This approach could have encouraged denial, as one voluntary sector worker re interviewed suggested: 'We are not tackling the very real problem of stereotyping by simply playing down the existence of the people who are unfortunate enough roughly to coincide with popular perception'.

Giving and taking help

Although social policy constraints leave social workers and probation officers unable to offer significant practical help to most clients who become homeless on leaving institutions, it is not good enough simply to blame the government and give up; we need to consider what values would underpin good practice. Methods for making contact with individuals beyond the stereotype and loosening clients' dependence on the homeless circuit of handouts and sub-standard accommodation, have been presented through case discussions by Oliver *et al.* (1989, ch. 15) and Jordan (1979, pp. 44–6). The authors recommend rejecting the 'presenting problem' or immediate request for a day's money or a bed for the night, in order to concentrate on the client's longer term predicament. This has the advantage of distinguishing the worker from all others who have sustained the client's progress around the circuit, and thereby gaining their attention. But it also devalues the reality of immediate, practical needs and therefore risks rejection in turn by the client.

It has become part of received professional wisdom (as stated, for example, by Hill & Laing, 1979) that social workers dislike giving 'material aid'. Insofar as this may be true, it probably derives from a wish to shed the old 'lady almoner' image and a fear of being exploited. While seeking to avoid use of money as the main currency in exchanges between worker and client, you should not be rigid about dispensing whatever cash and other material aid lies within your power. Don't be too proud to allow yourself to be conned now and then, if it makes a client feel good about scoring one over on the system! Living off the land is a social skill which homeless people need to acquire, and social work agencies form an important part of the territory.

It is only to be expected, for instance, that people with practically no money will convert any available assets into cash. In other circumstances it would be regarded as entrepreneurial to sell free clothes and furniture; yet some resettlement agencies prosecute clients who dispose of donated goods, thereby criminalising them (Dant & Deacon, 1989, p. 70). This is an over-reaction, placing undue value on relatively worthless, second-hand things above personal autonomy. Similarly it is unreasonable to punish clients for not accepting a hostel vacancy, or abandoning a tenancy which you have arranged for them, by withholding further help. While the rejection represents wasted effort on your part, the client may be right: perhaps they were not ready to move, or the placement was not suitable. Maybe you did it wrong and you can learn for next time how to make an offer of help more acceptable. In the meantime, client self-determination must be respected.

Successfully asking for help is as valuable a social skill as being able to offer it to others, as the researchers on leaving care concluded (cited above). Giving and seeking help are key elements in interpersonal relations, and are important aspects of empowerment for clients who are in the vulnerable position of needing help with basic necessities. But an undeclared moral code is often followed in social work, whereby clients are expected to ask for help; and to accept it even against their will (under statutory powers), but not just to take it. *Taking* help, on the client's own terms, is regarded as manipulative behaviour and that is feared by professionals in general because it undermines their power to give.

Some materialist inhibitions have to be overcome as a prerequisite for effective social work with marginalised homeless people. Perseverance and time are required, which may be hard to achieve for this purpose under case management systems.

Notes

1. Some of the general manuals on leaving home which are in the Resource List at the end of this book include: Clark & Dearling (1986); Coventry Young Homeless Project (1986); National Youth Agency (1991); Wright (1990). Children's Society (1991) is about young people leaving care. Housing Support Team (1992) is a detailed training manual for preparation courses.
2. See Note 1 to chapter 4 and Resource Information Service (1991, 2nd edition) in the Resource List.
3. Tenants or licensees of accommodation in HMOs have only limited legal protection from eviction, dangerous conditions and increases in rent, and what protection they have is often difficult to enforce. Campaign for Bedsit Rights (1991) explains what steps can be taken. Arden (1989) outlines the position for the sector in general, and Dowell *et al.* (1989) Part III.2 deals in detail with responses to harassment and illegal eviction. National Federation of Housing Associations (1991) is another general guide. All are entered in the Resource List.
4. A guide to improving medical services in the Resource List: National Federation of Housing Associations (1990).

3

Relationship Breakdown

The contribution of a couple's housing circumstances to the quality of their relationship has long been recognised. There are two aspects: where housing conditions themselves contribute to a deteriorating relationship; and the housing problems which may result afterwards. In this chapter we shall concentrate on the housing difficulties which follow relationship breakdown.

Limited income and lack of capital, associated with lower socio-economic class, can make it impossible for a couple who separate to sustain two homes and a comparable standard of living. Gender inequality and the patriarchal character of property ownership ensure that women are more likely than men to suffer consequent poverty and homelessness. Alternatively, women may be trapped in unhappy marriages because they have no prospect of finding somewhere else to live.

Discussion about social work roles in the housing problems stemming from relationship breakdown must first be contextualised within general demographic trends in British society: divorce, smaller households, and lone parenting. These three are partly related. First there is a general trend towards smaller households anyway, but the divorce rate – now in excess of one in three marriages – fuels both the smaller household trend and the increase to over one million in lone parent households, the vast majority of which are headed by women. As non-marital births have risen from 12.5 to 21 per cent of all births through the 1980s it is clear that there must be a large group of people with officially uncounted family

54

relationships – the stability of which is unknown (CSO, 1989). The only data indicating relationship breakdown that can be used with a reasonable degree of reliability are divorces (at 151 000 decrees absolute in England & Wales in 1987). However, the non-marital birth rate demonstrates that there is the potential for breakdown involving children which would not be recorded, except in cases where one of the separating parents applied to a court for access to the children (for discussion see Holmans in Symon, 1990, pp. 53–61).

Social work roles

Relationship breakdown is not unusual, nor, as Maclean argues, is it necessarily negative or problematic (1991, pp. 13–15). However it is unlikely that someone would approach a social work agency unless they were already in difficulty. Generalising from the evidence which will be cited in this chapter, it appears that while most separating couples do not contact social workers, a significant minority do; most commonly it is the woman, and the likelihood increases if there are dependent children and particularly if there has been violence.

Women usually rely for help initially on informal networks of family and friends. When these informal sources have run out, or the woman feels she can no longer impose on them, and the prospects of a secure income and permanent housing are no nearer, then she may contact a social worker – perhaps on a friend's recommendation, or referred by a GP. If the separation is violent and the woman and children leave in a crisis, she is more likely to go to a social work agency there and then, possibly on remembering a previous helpful contact over delayed benefit or a child care matter, for example, or referred by the police or a hospital casualty department. Women under probation supervision may contact their current or former probation officer in similar circumstances; but probation officers are more likely to encounter violence against women indirectly, when the man is their statutory client.

The methods and skills appropriate to working with people leaving broken relationships are varied, responding to different needs. *Protection* may be needed, from male violence, or from the destructive practices of housing officers in administering their homelessness procedures. Guidance on the NHS and Community Care Act gives welcome recognition to provision of refuges for abused women (DoH, 1990). Counselling may be used to *support* or sustain women through continuing, unresolved problems; and, on the other hand, to *confront* violent behaviour in men. Offering advice or information, undertaking advocacy and negotiating with other agencies and individuals – these skills are required in practically every situation which involves *access* to housing and other services. Actually *providing* things – furniture, transport, food, clothing – meets immediate practical needs when help from other agencies is not forthcoming, or seeking it through formal channels would be too stressful or time-consuming. We return to a general discussion of methods at the end of the chapter.

The values which social workers and probation officers follow in this area of practice must be anti-discriminatory. This means holding to a woman-centred approach (as advocated by Hanmer & Statham, 1988), whilst not denying the needs of any men involved, nor forgetting the vulnerability of children. These are complex issues. Women are most clearly the victims in broken relationships: victims of individual male partners and more generally of a patriarchal society, although social work agency policies have tended to give women in these circumstances rather low priority. But the other members of a former family have needs too, and are also more likely to be the statutory client: the man, in probation work, and children in local authority social work. Practitioners have to be aware of inherently conflicting demands.

In this chapter we consider the breakdown of relationships as a process, with options: first, one of the partners wants to leave. Then one or other of them takes the decision and does actually leave. It is important to distinguish between the woman leaving and the man leaving because the control over resources is different. Case examples are used, both to illustrate common situations and to suggest strategies. We should note that in these case examples, accommodation and financial problems were being described by psychiatric social workers, often as a context for other issues in their work with the clients concerned, which cannot be fully addressed here.

Wanting out

Using the term 'relationship breakdown' implies that there is an easily identified moment when one of the partners has decided that the relationship has ended. That is unusual. Particularly in a relationship of chronic violence, the woman may several times seek refuge from attack – some space and time to collect herself and decide on longer-term plans. The need for temporary shelter is real enough, even if in that instance it did not lead directly to permanent re-housing (Brailey, 1987, p. 41). Two tasks are paramount in social work involvement at this stage: arranging temporary accommodation, and support while thinking through the options.

During the process of splitting up, women turn to their own informal support network for immediate help. Friends and relatives provide the main source of emotional support and alternative accommodation. There is an expectation that the woman will find something permanent, soon, but it can be a drawn-out affair lasting years. The difficulties of imposing on relatives and friends are discussed by Brailey who lists:

> overcrowding, the need to watch and control your children in someone else's house, conflicting moral views on divorce, the danger of putting strain on relationships within the 'host' family itself, the need for independence, the awkwardness of sharing cooking facilities, arguments over money, the fear that the housing department would treat their application less urgently. (Brailey, 1987, pp. 39–40).

In that survey, about a half of the women turned to a welfare agency for support, believing strongly that 'people should not be expected to go to live with their parents or other relatives if their marriage breaks up'. But, as most women do turn initially to their relatives, it follows that those with few kin links will be more isolated and perhaps more dependent on social work agencies. In those circumstances, the social worker may be regarded as a 'substitute friend'.

However, before such a relationship could develop, a decision about leaving has to be taken. Many women in stressful relationships find it hard to make a firm decision that the partnership should end. Many hope the partner's response to them will change and they even tolerate violent behaviour in the hope that he will stop. An example is 53-year-old Mrs Beatty who has six children:

Client wishes to have flat for herself and youngest son, following matrimonial breakdown after many years of 'disharmony'. Borough council have been made aware of the situation. The next step is up to the client, insofar as continuing with divorce proceedings, should she fail to do so her chances of obtaining council property in her own right are nil. The only problem is that she has got to this stage before and backed out. If court were to turn the house over to her, client doesn't wish this as she wouldn't be able to pay for repairs and upkeep and wishes to live in a smaller property. The client has been offered accommodation by her children, but she doesn't wish to move in with them.

The decision to be taken is clearly not just about ending the relationship. As in so many cases, Mrs Beatty is financially dependent on her husband; and even making a claim for income support is unlikely to be successful while she is still living under the same roof. Separate claims are technically possible, but they would have to show that their daily lives were being conducted independently, which at the very least requires a high degree of co-operation.

Few women in Mrs Beatty's circumstances would have sufficient independent income to buy a property, or for a deposit on the expensive sort of private tenancy where children are accepted; so the only possibility is public renting. A woman with dependent children and subject to violence would probably be allocated a tenancy; either one condition or the other might lead to rehousing eventually. Differences in treatment will probably reflect each local housing authority's available stock, despite Code of Guidance admonishments to equal treatment (Brailey, 1987, p. 39 DoE, 1991B, para. 6.17). But many councils would expect the woman to leave and become homeless before they would do anything, particularly if the situation had already arisen before, as with Mrs Beatty. And they would then tell her to move in with those adult children who had offered accommodation, where she would be regarded as adequately housed. A social worker's negotiating strategy could aim to have the housing department accept the woman and youngest child as homeless, on the grounds of marital breakdown (divorce proceedings should not be required), and for one of the adult children to accommodate them temporarily as an alternative to being placed in temporary accommodation. Their rehousing rights would not be affected and they would be spared the stress of a prolonged stay in B & B. The arrangement should be more acceptable to all concerned if it is known to be temporary, but that would be convincing only if the housing department put it in writing.

In the case of Mrs Goddard the sympathies of helping agencies seem to lie with her husband, who has multiple sclerosis, rather than with her, the client, who is described as a 'volatile Italian, not suited to crushing burden of handicapped husband'. There is also a 17-year-old daughter living at home and said by her mother to be 'acting up'; an older son left to join the armed forces.

House unsuitable for care of almost totally handicapped man. Wife behaves as if he were normal. Not possible to solve problem except by organising vastly inflated price for own house and making exchange for purpose-built bungalow, which in turn would exacerbate relationship problems. Approached council and housing association for purpose built accommodation – all refused by client. All agencies have been exceptionally helpful. The client has been persistently obstructive. Wants release from sick husband.

Seven years of social work have apparently done little to help this woman adjust to 'loss of expectation in marriage' and accept her alternative allotted female role as carer.

Separation seems to be the fairest solution, for which the woman had expressed a preference. The house could be sold and its value split, the man going into rented, sheltered housing with home nursing care (until his money ran out, which would be a problem for future negotiation with relevant charities) and the woman making her own way in private renting. At least she would be free; but we are not told what he thinks about it all. The case illustrates conflict between several anti-discriminatory principles; one is equality of opportunity for a woman, possibly at the expense of a man with a severe disability (without a live-in carer he may go into residential care). Also there is an ethnic dimension, in the racial stereotyping of the woman, who has also acquired disabled status as a psychiatric patient. The social worker's priority must be the woman who is her client; but there is also some responsibility to ensure that the man has an advocate.

Having taken the decision, who leaves? There are three possibilities: the woman leaves and the man stays; the man leaves and the woman stays; they both leave separately. An indication of the distribution between these three can be gathered from various research studies. In one national survey of owner occupiers the woman left initially in 33 per cent of cases, the man in 44 per cent, and they both left in 23 per cent (Dodd & Hunter, 1990, table 2.20, p. 13). In a survey of divorced couples in Scotland, overall men were slightly less likely to leave the matrimonial home than women, but if the house were owner-occupied, the men were much more likely to stay (Jackson in Symon, 1990, pp. 79–80). Another Scottish study found that more than two-thirds of respondents were not in the matrimonial home three years after divorce (Wasoff & Dobash in Symon ed., 1990, p. 144). These studies confirm and expand on Sullivan's earlier work: half of all women move out of the marital home on separation or divorce, of which more than 40 per cent have children. A further fifth of those who remain then also move within a year (Sullivan, 1986).

The question who leaves first is difficult to answer; perhaps the best generalisation is that the partner taking responsibility for the children, the 'custodial mother', is highly likely to leave with them, a finding which flies in the face of received wisdom (Wasoff & Dobash in Symon, 1990, pp. 148–9). But even that bold move of leaving does not have a neat outcome because if there is nowhere to go, people have to make 'interim arrangements' which develop an air of permanence as time passes.

The woman leaves

When women decide to leave, what tends to be 'visible' to researchers and practitioners alike are the unsatisfactory and unresolved outcomes of relationship breakdown. Apart from those who re-marry, we ignore, or rather are unable to quantify, women who form new relationships, or are happy to be single and better-off on their own.

Women take the initiative in divorce. As almost three-quarters of divorce petitions are filed by the wife, this may be an indication that the husband left her; but half the decrees granted to women were on the grounds of their husband's 'unreasonable behaviour', suggesting that she had left or manoeuvred him out (from *Social Trends*, nos 20 & 21, 1990 & 91). Among the women who leave, the largest single group move into rented accommodation via relatives or friends (two-thirds in the research cited below). The period following separation is characterised by profound instability and mobility, which seems to stabilise just before the actual divorce. Although there was no gender difference in the rate at which men and women moved into shared accommodation, their respective experiences were very different, mainly because most women moved with their children whereas most men did not (Wasoff & Dobasah, p. 153; the findings of Jackson, p. 80. are similar, both in Symon, 1990).

Whatever sector their previous home, many women end up renting from public authorities: one study found 58 per cent of women applying for public housing (Jackson in Symon ed., 1990, p. 80). Half of all divorced and separated women who are 'head' of their own household are council tenants (OPCS, 1986, table 5.16). This includes women who were living in council tenancies to start with, of whom less than a fifth moved on divorce and nearly another third later, probably transferring within the public sector (Sullivan, 1986).

In those parts of the country where two-thirds or more of the population are already owner-occupiers and new council building has more or less ceased, separating couples have little choice but to remain indefinitely with relatives or in private lodgings, or to move down market in owner occupation. DoE (1991A fig. 67 p. 85) shows just 14000 local authority completions in 1989, after a decade of steady decline. In assessing the demand for additional housing created by divorce, Holmans estimates 40000 pa for owner-occupation; additionally 30000 pa for public rented housing, or 15 per cent of the 200000 public rented relets a year (in Symon, 1990, p. 73). Dodd and Hunter (1990, table 2.23, p. 14) provide evidence for the move to smaller property following break-up. The divorced women in McCarthy and Simpson's study described graphically the poor quality of the housing to which they had moved, in unfamiliar, and usually worse, surroundings without supportive networks (in Symon, 1990, pp. 184–5).

Buying at the bottom of the market can mean taking on the burden of maintaining a substandard house which is also decreasing in value. In the following example Ms Nicholson left a husband, but then found herself trapped in owner-occupation which was both too expensive and provided inadequate living conditions. Building societies are so keen for business that they will give mortgages even to lone parents in part-time work who cannot really afford the repayments. As her social worker said, she:

> holds down responsible job . . . Present house in a mess – cause of depression in addition to other causes. Lives in a very old dilapidated house, not good saleable prospect and carries substantial mortgage. Cannot afford to have it done up. Approached housing associations to buy house. Refused at present. Very low priority for council housing as is owner of house.

In the example of Ms O'Shaughnessy the situation is carried to the next stage. After splitting-up she bought another house but then got a council flat, with social work help. She had a part-time job, and two sons aged 7 and 13 from whom she was separated.

Client . . . had been conned into buying very substandard property using for a deposit the lump sum from property settlement after divorce . . . Youngest child had been taken into care. Great difficulty in persuading LA to allocate this client a flat as she was an owner occupier but was in severe financial trouble. Could not keep up with mortgage payments and maintenance, repairs etc . . . Can cope very well in two bedroom flat on third floor of a high rise tower. LA were co-operative in allowing her a two bedroom flat so that her children could visit and stay.

In that case it appears that the woman is content where she is; but for others, the isolation of high rise living, combined with continued separation from children, could have worsened rather than lifted depression.

The man leaves

The woman's near-impossible search for somewhere comparable to live with her children can be avoided if her husband will move out instead. It is not surprising that, given their position of relative power and control over financial resources, most men seem reluctant to surrender occupation unless they are planning to move in with another woman somewhere else. Excluding a man from his home when he will not leave turns on whether there has been domestic violence. Mrs Irving's case illustrates the use of injunctions which are often presented as the most effective way of excluding men:

In hospital at time of referral. Seeking injunction to remove spouse form council flat. Refused to return upon discharge if husband not removed. Client was granted injunction and husband left. Client returned home to be with her children.

For a court to grant an injunction in these circumstances Mr Irving must already have been violent to his wife; he could not otherwise be required to leave, as both partners are protected by the Matrimonial Homes Act 1983. But in order to prove grounds for an 'ouster order' the woman must place herself at risk of violence or remain homeless (Watchman in Symon, 1990, p. 96). The protection of that Act also has the effect of making both spouses permanently secure council tenants under the Housing Act 1980, until any property settlement on divorce.[1] This follows recommendations by the Scottish Law Commission (1980: see also Tuckley, 1985; GLC, 1985).

Scottish courts now have the power to transfer the tenancy at an abused woman's request, and the housing authority must rehouse the displaced partner. It is proving an inappropriate and ineffective remedy. All the difficulties which a woman faces in moving out herself seem to be outweighed by those of a tenancy transfer, exclusion of the man and his re-housing elsewhere. Some housing departments have used an application for transfer to attempt a 'reconciliation' so they can avoid allocating another tenancy. Sometimes women had the tenancy transferred, but the men were not rehoused and there did not seem to be a practical way of excluding them from their former home. Watchman concludes that the interaction of homelessness, domestic violence and matrimonial law in Scotland 'has tended not to increase the housing options available to women but to undermine the rights of homeless women' (in Symon, 1990, p. 95; also Jackson, in Symon, 1990, pp. 87–9; Brailey, 1987, pp. 42–4; One Plus, 1988, p. 30).

Social workers should beware of relying on legal remedies against domestic violence; they may not work, and measures which were intended to protect women can make them more vulnerable. Thus practitioners should hesitate to recommend an injunction as a woman's only form of protection, and never penalise her for drawing the same conclusion herself. A report from Tower Hamlets social services describes how seven children were received into 'voluntary' care because their mother had been leaving them on their own. She was frightened that their father would come and beat her up again so she used to go out at night to avoid him (Wilkinson, 1983, p. 83). An injunction was little help in this situation, even with powers of arrest attached, because of police reluctance to become involved in 'domestic disputes' and the courts' willingness to accept men's assurances of good behaviour (Binney *et al.*, 1981, pp. 14–18; Police Monitoring and Research Group, 1986, pp. 27–8; McGibbon *et al.*, 1989, pp. 100–1). In the late 1980s some police forces attempted to change working procedures in this area, but it remains to be seen whether changes in attitudes and practices will follow.

Sometimes men deliberately engineer a situation whereby their former partner is made homeless, even after they have left, as in the case of a woman whose

> house was damaged by fire in which client was severely injured. Sold by husband while she was in hospital. Though divorced, he had allowed her to stay in it. Made homeless by ex-husband.

Mrs Carruthers, a former nurse, was living on income support with her three teenage children in a house rented from a new town development corporation. Her social worker described what happened about eighteen months previously:

> Family made homeless by husband setting fire to marital home (owner-occupied) after being divorced. Much social work involvement at time of crisis. Client, although very distressed, did make her own arrangements to stay with relatives. She was known to this department before the actual trauma of losing her home. Had been referred as anxiety state due to deteriorating marital relationship and the implication of the disharmony for the children. Husband eventually convicted of arson and sentenced to imprisonment. At the time the problems were great as it all happened in December with winter climate and a few days prior to Christmas.

That woman was already on the caseload and received considerable on-going social work support, but seems to have made the practical arrangements herself. Mrs Archard contacted the hospital team as a last resort after trying other agencies to no avail:

> Husband left marital home which was then being bought with a mortgage and sold it over his wife's head. She was

given notice to quit. Continually harassed and pressurised.
Client had sought help from area team, solicitor and
applied for local authority housing. Housed by housing
association after application by hospital social worker. I
managed to involve extended family in practical tasks
(moving furniture) and emotional support.

Academic and practitioner research is inconclusive about
the effectiveness of social workers in responding to abused
women, and some researchers are highly critical. We need to
evaluate the evidence on social work and male violence and
consider possible explanations, with a view to reinforcing
good practice. When the violence is public, it seems that
social workers respond positively to the crisis, providing
support, protection and practical help, and that women value
their contribution more than that of other agencies. But when
abuse is private and routine, it may remain un-noticed by
social workers who are slow, or possibly reluctant, to draw
conclusions from the obvious signs. Help will usually be given
to a woman and children who have left a violent home, but
not to those who remain. This suggests that it is homelessness,
legitimated by violence, which triggers help, not the violence
alone (Smith, 1989, reviews the evidence, pp. 76, 82–3).

Gender differences are implied in a Hammersmith study
which found some female social workers more aware than
male of the domestic violence in the lives of their clients.
When a woman started by asking about child care or a
housing issue, female social workers were more likely than
their male colleagues to probe further and discover the
underlying problem of violence. The researchers concluded
that many social workers avoid confronting the issue of male
violence against women by concentrating on 'the children' or
retreating into sexist and racist stereotypes (McGibbon *et al.*,
1989, pp. 58–60). Possibly a threatening subject was being
kept at a distance by engaging only with the 'presenting
problem'. The findings of this study indicate that women
social workers should normally do duty work and conduct
intake interviews with women clients (though in some teams
that would leave male workers with little to do!).

In a national study for Women's Aid, women living in refuges said that a quarter of the social workers whom they had approached for help suggested reconciliation, and that they should not leave, 'for the sake of the children' (Binney *et al.*, 1981, p. 19). Such advice may have been based on a realistic appraisal of women's housing prospects, but it was interpreted as being unsympathetic and was evidently not heeded. Local authority social workers are expected to give priority to children's needs, but those are unlikely to be served by living in a violent home, and it is both insensitive and counter-productive to give an abused woman the impression that she deserves help only as a mother, not as an individual.

One researcher concluded that the social workers whose casenotes she analysed were 'neutral' towards domestic violence and that their attitude 'constitutes a working patriarchy . . . [and] illustrates how the state upholds male domination, control and the policing of women' (Maynard in Pahl, 1985, p. 140; similarly Swain, 1986, on probation work). This indictment is not upheld by current observation in many social work agencies, where practitioners are increasingly aware of anti-discrimination issues. Even in the past there have been some outstanding examples of good practice in social work with abused women (Pahl, 1978, pp. 43–5; Pahl, 1985, pp. 80–94, 160–3; Binney *et al.*, 1981, pp. 19–20; Clark & Huckle, 1986).

More than half of the women surveyed in refuges were satisfied with the help they had received from social workers, which mainly concerned housing and other practical problems. But as the Hammersmith researchers remarked, practitioners are not generally supported in this type of work within their organisations and appropriate local information systems are often lacking (McGibbon *et al.*, 1989, pp. 63–5). Many social services departments have declared an equal opportunities policy. Part of this would mean regarding the women as a client in her own right. Managers must understand that implementing such a policy requires giving an operational priority to aspects of practical social work which tend not to feature in Department of Health guidance and have hitherto been downgraded.

Problems the man has left behind

As the man may leave behind financial problems which the woman has to live with but finds difficult to solve, it is worth investigating arrears and debts at this point.

Rent arrears and fuel debts which have been building up for some time may come to a woman's notice only after her husband leaves. Just as poor housing conditions may be both a contributing factor to relationship breakdown and a consequence, so may debt. Allowing debts to mount can be a man's response to a deteriorating relationship, failure to pay bills being an expression of the low value he attaches to his family life. Similarly prior to separation men often allow the house to fall into extreme disrepair, leaving their partner with expensive renovation work, or greatly lowering the equity value.[2]

Women with violent partners may find that they lack access to household resources. A tenancy can slip into arrears because the woman fears abuse if she tries to get more money off her partner to pay the rent (Welsh Women's Aid, 1986, p. 35). Where debt is caused by reduced income of which both partners are aware, the associated anxiety can itself contribute to deterioration in their relationship. Mrs Jennings had been quite unaware of her husband's activities, although so-called 'non-acquiescence' in a partner's illegal activities is very difficult to establish legally (Watchman in Symon, 1990, pp. 101–2): 'Accommodation was near to becoming a crisis when client in danger of eviction through massive rent arrears etc. following husband being sentenced to three years imprisonment'. Her social worker helped to avert disaster by, 'direct debiting, crisis work, help with budgeting; liaison with DHSS, probation service, school, playgroup'.

A wife in Mrs Jennings' situation is not legally responsible for arrears of rent which have been accumulated without her knowledge, if the tenancy is in her husband's name, but this will not necessarily deter the council landlord from threatening action against her (Tuckley, 1985, pp. 11–12). Housing department attitudes in allocating the rent arrears following relationship breakdown vary widely from attributing the total arrears to the remaining partner, to apportioning them equally (Bull & Stone, 1990). The social worker helping Mrs Jennings took action across the range of possibilities, doubtless because of the imminence of eviction and family breakdown that might ensue.

Another and separate aspect of financial difficulty involves maintenance. Of course such trouble may arise whether the woman has left or stayed. Mrs Knox stayed; she was divorced with two teenage children, working full-time and living with a new partner in the former matrimonial home, for which she still paid the mortgage. Relations with her partner were not good; the hospital social worker wrote: 'At one stage accommodation threatened to be a problem as she was in danger of not being able to afford to stay in present home due to financial problems (husband not paying maintenance, etc.), however parents rallied to her support'. Had this not happened, possible remedies would have depended on complicated terms of the maintenance and property settlement which was made at the time she was divorced.[3]

Mortgage arrears

Given the organising principles of this book it is difficult to find a satisfactory logical location for a section on mortgage arrears. But find a place we must, for the incidence of home loss due to mortgage arrears is increasing at a much higher rate than the owner-occupied sector is expanding.

Since 1980 yearly repossessions by building societies have multiplied thirteen-fold. At 43 890 repossessions, 1990 had a total two-thirds higher than the previously highest year, 1987 (Council of Mortgage Lenders, 1991). Local authority lenders are less likely than building societies to evict mortgage defaulters but more likely to take them to court routinely (AMA, 1986B, pp. 31–3) and have no less of a financially motivated approach to recovery of the debt (Doling *et al.*, 1986; Doling & Wainwright, 1989). Women are particularly vulnerable after relationship breakdown, because of their sudden decline in total income and the high likelihood of previously incurred arrears. A local study in Glasgow found more than a third of defaulting families to be lone parents (Purkiss and Sim, 1985, p. 11). Dodd and Hunter have shown that 27 per cent of owner-occupiers who moved had financial difficulties, the main one of which was paying the mortgage (1990, p. 19).

The example of Mr and Mrs Mills will help us to examine the practicalities of mortgage repayment and the potential for relationship breakdown. Mr Mill's social worker described him as in a: 'Chronic anxiety state – given up work which he feels is unsuitable. Fighting to save marriage. Wife has multiple sclerosis and is deteriorating'. Although Mr and Mrs Mills' problems related mainly to their relationship and the wife's chronic sickness, there was also a danger that they could have fallen into mortgage arrears. In their early thirties, they were paying off a recent mortgage on a suburban house, their only income being his unemployment benefit and her part-time earnings which were not likely to last as her health deteriorated. If they became entitled to income support, the mortgage interest repayments would be met in full after 16 weeks, but only 50 per cent initially. That would leave arrears to be made up from some other source.

Social workers must be alert to the risk of mortgage arrears and be able to advise clients how to avert home loss. In the long term, paying a mortgage is usually incompatible with continuing unemployment. Capital repayments are not allowable under social security regulations, so they can be made only at the expense of basic living requirements such as food. But mortgage interest payments can be met from income support. If the lender will renegotiate the terms of the mortgage to reduce monthly payments for a while, this can prevent arrears accumulating and allow time for the client to look for another job or sort out her maintenance (The *Rights Guide to Home Owners* advises what to do). Lenders do not have to be helpful, however, and a government survey of claimants with mortgages found that in a quarter of cases the lender, usually a building society, had refused to negotiate (SSPI, 1986, paras 2.29, 6.6, table A.13). A more recent study found that only 7 per cent of those with arrears had their loan rescheduled (Dodd & Hunter, 1990, p. 25). A further problem arises from the Child Support Act which makes absent fathers pay for the maintenance of their children, thus potentially undermining existing arrangements where the father contributes instead to the mortgage of the former matrimonial home until the children come of age (HoC Social Security Committee, 1991).

What happens to the man?

Surprisingly it appears that most people do not consider the housing consequences of relationship breakdown prior to leaving (Jackson in Symon, 1990, p. 82). So if the man leaves he probably will not have arranged anything and will have real difficulties in finding suitable permanent accommodation. However men who leave do not usually take the children with them, hence it is considerably easier for them to find private rented accommodation, admittedly a sector of insecurity and poor conditions. That may be easy, but it is near impossible for them to gain priority for council housing. Owner-occupation is not usually possible until the former matrimonial home is sold, when they too will doubtless have to trade down market (Dodd & Hunter, 1990, table 2.23, p. 16). Local authority social workers are only likely to have such single men on their caseloads if mental illness or physical disability are involved, but it is more likely in probation work.

Staying with parents is the typical outcome for the man who leaves with nowhere else to go and is illustrated by Mr Quayle, whose wife had custody of their two young children. After moving 'many times' between privately rented bedsits, he lived in his parents' high rise council flat and claimed income support. Mr Quayle's social worker said he had been admitted to hospital several times in the past couple of years, being treated for depression and drug abuse. He was described as 'semi-literate, unreliable, budgeting problems – finds it hard to find the rent'.

Mr Quayle's route to his parents was via bedsits; another possibility can be a hostel placement. Mr Robinson aged 50 and divorced was also unemployed:

Lives with elderly father-in-law in cramped conditions. Client spent some time in hostel then returned to live with father-in-law. Reason given was financial. Refuses further offers of hostel accommodation. Client has placed himself on LA housing list. Says he is happy to remain where he is until allocated LA flat.

The hostel placement was being offered as a solution both to overcrowding and to support needs but was judged inappropriate by Mr Robinson on financial grounds.

Single men may try to make a home with whichever relatives will have them, illustrated by the two following examples. Social workers had probably become involved because of the 'alcoholism' of Mr Sowerby, aged 43, divorced, unemployed:

> Living with aunt – overcrowding. Would like council flat but has been refused as he has substantial rent arrears from a previous tenancy. Client is hoping to borrow money from relatives to repay arrears.

Mr Townsend was 62 and lived with one of his four married children in a council house:

> After being divorced by wife had to leave marital home. Went into lodgings. Started to drink heavily. Physical state declining rapidly. Could not manage on his own – dietary deficiencies etc . . . Client now living with son and family. Arrangement appears to be working well.

Although it was probably not difficult to obtain lodgings for Mr Townsend, he was clearly unhappy. It is usual for relatives to respond helpfully at least in the initial stages. The last example illustrates that if relatives accept the situation, a 'temporary' arrangement may become permanent. Mr Townsend might be regarded as 'vulnerable because of old age', otherwise these men have low priority for council housing.

Interim arrangements

Major difficulties experienced at relationship breakdown revolve around keeping a right to live in the former marital home and alternatively, getting access to council housing. But women often make contact with social workers at an in-between stage, when they are staying temporarily with relatives, friends or in lodgings, as two-thirds do. When these interim arrangements continue longer than expected, with no resolution in sight, divorced and separated mothers may seek the help of a formal agency which they would not otherwise have approached (Parsons, 1983). A small survey by Henderson and Argyle (1985) found that half the women they interviewed had contacted a social worker at some time during the six months after separation, that is when most were making their 'interim arrangements'.

With relatives

A bed in someone else's house is all that most women with children can hope to get at short notice, anything else being too difficult of access (if public) or much too expensive (if private). 22-year-old Ms Phillip's position is common:

> In need of flat for herself and child following break-up of marriage – conflict and overcrowding at parental home. Awaiting outcome of court proceedings – may be reinstated in marital home. If court finds in her favour, housing dept. should find her accommodation – if not then will have difficulties as technically has a place to live with parents.

One should challenge the 'technicality' of having a place to live – there is overcrowding and conflict in what probably began as a charitable temporary arrangement until she got sorted out. Ms Phillip's predicament is one commonly exploited by local authority homelessness officers to avoid accepting responsibility for rehousing under homelessness legislation.

Sometimes the social worker must consider a number of factors, each affecting housing opportunity in a different way. Mrs Talbot, mother of a severely handicapped four-year-old child, was using the spare room of a friend's flat in which to care for her daughter:

Marriage broke-up due to husband's unreasonable behaviour and wife (client) left marital home with daughter. Stayed with friends. Case transferred to social worker involved with handicapped child as housing needs very much reflected the special needs of child and its future care.

To some extent the social work and housing issues are similar to those in the case of Mrs Goddard, where a decision had to be taken on whether the interests of someone with a disability should take precedence over those of the original client. In the example of Mrs Talbot, solving the special housing needs of the daughter should also solve those of her mother, as the decision to leave the matrimonial home had already been taken, but she was trapped in a poor interim arrangement. Ignoring the housing problem in this case could result in a crisis later when the tolerance of friends ran out.

Making an assessment of a client's situation which is sensitive to the whole range of their needs and aspirations is the first skill which a social worker must develop. Assessment should be done with the client at every stage, both as a matter of principle, to counter possibly long-standing discrimination and promote empowerment, and of pragmatism, to facilitate the client's co-operation in future planning. Thereafter provision of information, advice and advocacy is likely to be consistent to most cases, the emphasis changing with the circumstances. Networking skills, directed at involving a client's relatives and other potential supporters, may be appropriate for people who have become socially isolated; but experience suggests that, when couples split up, both partners turn to their relatives and are likely to contact formal agencies only after exhausting their own informal networks.

Social work with women leaving bad relationships may be characterised by crisis intervention, focused on getting the family through a weekend of homelessness and hunger; or longer term support to sustain them through a period of little improvement and declining spirits. In either case the achievement of substantial material change, in the form of permanent rehousing, may be beyond the competence of ordinary social workers, but the forms of help which practitioners can offer are much valued by clients.

Notes

1. SHAC's guides to the rights of married and cohabiting women explain how to obtain an injunction: see Resource List – Witherspoon, 1989, and McNicholas, 1989; also, in less detail, chapter 6 of Randall, 1989, *Housing Rights Guide* and, in full detail, part I of Dowell *et al.*, 1989 *The Emergency Procedures Handbook*. *Making the Break* by two women's aid workers offers the best general advice to women experiencing domestic violence, applicable to Scotland and Northern Ireland as well as England and Wales, though partially superseded by S11 of the Housing (Scotland) Act 1986 and expected homelessness legislation in Northern Ireland (Carew-Jones and Watson, 1985). For general advice *Women's Housing Handbook: England and Wales* is a readable guide (Resource Information Service, 1988). *Love and Pain* is also specifically for women, addressing the emotional issues of abusing relationships and their breakdown, while suggesting practical remedies (Horley, 1988). Scottish Women's Aid produce a guide to the Scottish legislation. The National Council for One Parent Families have produced a practical and readable *Information Manual: Guide to Rights Benefits and Services for Lone Parents*. All these guides are in the Resource List.
2. The evidence for these conclusions is discussed by McCarthy & Simpson, pp. 182–3 and Wasoff & Dobash, p. 156 both in Symon, 1990; and Maclean, 1991, p. 22 on irresponsible husbands and family obligations.
3. Unreliable maintenance is a particular worry for owner occupiers; Ennals *et al.*, 1990 (see Resource List) advise how it can be avoided. A woman with earned income whose maintenance payments have become irregular may be entitled to family credit which provides some compensation, as the CPAG *National Welfare Benefits Handbook* explains. Note that the implementation of the Child Support Act 1991 will change this radically.

4

Homeless Families

In examining relationship breakdown, and in particular domestic violence, we found that homelessness was the likely outcome in many cases. Applying to the local authority housing department as homeless often seemed to be the only housing solution available. Homeless applicants are treated differently depending on household composition and those most likely to be helped are adults with dependent children: 'homeless families'.[1] Social services have statutory child care and protection duties, hence in the crisis-ridden and stressful world of homelessness it is to be expected that social workers may become involved. However Britain's chronic homelessness has a history, featuring social work in what has been presented as a rather negative role. We need to consider the reasons for these developments in order to make sense of social work with homeless families as it emerged during the 1980s.

Social work's historical involvement

Local authority welfare departments were responsible for accommodating homeless families, under a residual provision in Part III of the National Assistance Act 1948, until specific legislation made that a housing department responsibility in 1977. Homelessness during the post-war period in Britain moved from being a welfare issue towards redefinition in terms of housing need. Dealing with homelessness had become increasingly problematic and social work involvement with homeless families came under criticism from many quarters. Academic critiques suggested that social services' continuing responsibility for homelessness contributed to families with housing problems being labelled inappropriately as deviants (for example, Minns, 1972).

There was little if any practice literature about what social workers with the homeless actually did under the old welfare departments. Seebohm had recommended that lead responsibility for dealing with homelessness should be transferred to housing departments and that where social work help was required, 'This should be provided by the social service department on the same basis as for other families living in their own houses' (Seebohm, 1968, para. 405).

Slowness in implementing that policy change was said to have been a cause of dissatisfaction among practitioners in the new social services departments during the 1970s. Social workers had the unenviable task of responding to a problem whose solution required a resource – housing – over which they had no control. It was unpopular work and they were said to have 'breathed a sigh of relief' when legal responsibility was transferred in 1977 (Cooper, 1980, pp. 79–80; Kent, 1981, para. 5.1; May & Whitbread, 1975; Satyamurti, 1981; Stevenson & Parsloe, 1978, pp. 36, 369–70).

Housing leads a corporate responsibility

The Housing (Homeless Persons) Act, 1977, placed a corporate responsibility on local authorities to make provision for homeless people in defined circumstances. While the main duties lay with housing departments, social services departments were under a duty to co-operate and the Codes of Guidance which have accompanied the Act stress the importance of co-operation (latest version: DoE *et al.*, 1991B, ch. 15). The separate Scottish Code of Guidance was expressed more strongly: 'effective and speedy co-operation is of paramount importance in the implementation of the Act . . . It is important to avoid an unnecessarily restrictive view of the duties and responsibilities of social work/housing departments respectively in relation to homeless people' (Scottish Development Department, 1980, paras 7.5–7.6). The Scottish approach was supported by recommendations from the Morris Committee (1975) on joint working between housing and social work in Scotland.

The 1977 Act may seem like an attempt by two central government departments to impose collaboration upon the two local authority departments concerned, but the policy was by no means new. There had been similar exhortations to co-operate made in earlier circulars, all of which were jointly issued at central government level. A circular issued by the Departments of the Environment and of Health and Social Security, in 1974, stated that: 'The prevention and relief of homelessness is a function of local government as a whole and not of either housing authorities or social services authorities alone. Only a corporate and collaborative approach . . . can . . . span the range of needs of the homeless and ensure that they are met . . . by realising the full resources of local government. The homeless are not a category whose problems can be classified simply by reference to the responsibility of a particular authority or department' (para. 13).

A private member's bill, which was adopted by the Wilson government's 'Lib/Lab pact', became the Housing (Homeless Persons) Act 1977, to bring into line the one-third of local housing authorities (mainly in the shires) which had not implemented the 1974 circular. The content of the 1977 Act was recodified into Part III of the Housing Act 1985 but that did not signify acceptance into the housing mainstream. Homelessness remained marginal to government policy; it was not even mentioned in a white paper on housing (DoE, 1987) and there was a real possibility that the specific legislation would be repealed following a review just ten years after its introduction.

Officially recorded levels of homelessness have risen every year, from 53 110 households for England in 1978 to 145 800 in 1990: a tripling over eleven years. Problems with the Department of the Environment's quarterly statistics – inconsistent criteria, incomplete returns – make detailed examination of the figures unhelpful for the present purpose, but such analyses are available elsewhere (for example, National Audit

Office, 1990A). Some 80 per cent of those accepted are families with dependent children or expecting their first baby, half being lone parents (Evans & Duncan, 1988, pp. 3, 43). In this chapter we concentrate on homeless families with dependent children, having discussed the single homeless in chapter 2.

Research into homelessness conducted during the 1980s was very much housing orientated; a social work perspective was scarcely considered, nor was much attention paid to the contribution of social services departments. Any mention of social services was usually brief and often critical: for example, as a source of pressure on housing departments; as one of a range of services which is unavailable to homeless families; as creators of homelessness by discharging young people from care and 'vulnerable' adults from institutions. The neglect of social work issues by housing researchers into homelessness reflects a general paucity of academic literature on relations between housing and social services departments (noted by Hudson, 1986).

Within the profession, leading social services spokespersons have kept a low profile on the subject of homeless families. The Chief Social Services Inspector said: 'The Department of Health has no direct responsibility for family homelessness, but does see that it has a role in persuading the Department of the Environment to alleviate the problem' (Utting in Social Services Inspectorate, 1989A, p. 4). The Association of Metropolitan Authorities, whose members carry both social services and housing responsibilities, made only a passing reference to social workers in its report on homelessness, mentioning them on a par with health visitors who are, of course, employed by health authorities (AMA, 1990, p. 12). A Code of Practice on social services support for families in temporary accommodation, which was adopted by the London branch of the Association of Directors of Social Services and the Association of London Authorities, noted that: 'In making any social services provision authorities must always bear in mind that *homelessness is primarily a housing problem* and that anything done by social services can only alleviate the symptoms of the problem' (ADSS, 1985, para. 3.1; original emphasis).

Specialist practitioners with homeless families

Our own research has shown that despite such cautious distancing specialist social work with homeless people was expanding during the period following the 1977 Act, mainly in newly established fieldwork settings. One of the social workers whom we interviewed described what happened as, 'a sudden spate of specialist social work teams working with both single and family homeless', which had followed from a period of contraction in social services activity after the 1974 circular. She added: 'It would be pleasing to think this was a belated effort at a corporate approach to homelessness but it is more likely to reflect the social work reaction on behalf of those groups of people excluded from priority housing provision' (the interviews referred to in this chapter are analysed more fully in Stewart & Stewart, 1992A).

An emerging interest in homelessness among national social work organisations during the mid-1980s offered the possibility that a support structure would develop for these specialists and for generic practitioners in areas where homeless families were concentrated (BASW, 1986; Social Services Inspectorate, 1989B, p. 5). However this proved to be London-centric and dominated by voluntary organisations. More voluntary sector staff than local authority social workers attended a study day on family homelessness which was organised by the Social Services Inspectorate in 1987, and the Chief Inspector reinforced this imbalance in an address to a follow-up event two years later. Comparing the statutory sector unfavourably to the voluntary sector, he suggested that local authority social work was inflexible, stigmatising and threatening to families who feared that their children might be removed (Utting in SSI, 1989A, pp.8–9). In the 1990s, social workers with homeless families remain somewhat professionally isolated.

Preventing homelessness

Statutory homelessness is a process. First there is the application to the Homeless Persons' Unit (HPU) of the housing department with its investigations and possible rejection; next a period in temporary accommodation; finally rehousing, which we examine in chapter 5. Although this is becoming the normal route into public housing, the latter is not guaranteed and the homelessness procees can feel like an obstacle course for the families going through it. In the following sections we shall examine how and why social workers become involved and how agencies differ in their practices.

The Codes of Guidance place most emphasis on co-operation in the area of prevention: 'Housing and social work departments should work out agreed policies and procedures to prevent homelessness. Whenever either a housing or social work authority becomes aware of the possibility of homelessness occurring they should alert the other to the circumstances without delay' (SDD, 1980, para. 7.7a; DoE *et al.*, 1991B, para. 10.2). However it is necessary to examine the different meanings of prevention in order to assess how far they are compatible in practice. We shall find that each agency has a different expectation of what 'preventing homelessness' might involve.

One specific expectation from the housing side is that social workers should assist in the recovery of rent arrears and give rent guarantees in order to avoid eviction, on the grounds that rent arrears are often a symptom of personal and financial difficulties (DoE *et al.*, 1991B, paras 10.5, 10.6e, 10.14 & 15.4). Social workers tend to reject the role of rent collector, regarding that as the housing department's job. On the other hand, it is appropriate to help families with benefit and debt problems, and arrangements may be useful whereby social services is notified of impending evictions so that the family can be visited or someone such as a welfare rights officer can attend the court. However eviction of tenants for any reason declined as a cause of homelessness during the 1980s, being overtaken by mortgage foreclosure; and there is no suggestion in the Codes of Guidance that social workers should become involved with owner-occupiers.

The second area in which social services co-operation is expected concerns 'domestic disputes', which are the most common single official cause of homelessness. Social workers may be asked to 'assess . . . the severity of the dispute' and to 'offer counselling and casework support . . . directed towards relieving tension within the household so as to enable the members to continue to live together' (DoE *et al.*, 1991B, para. 10.23; SDD, 1980, para. 3.11). The DoE's survey of local authority policies found that social services were often called upon to make assessments of 'domestic disputes'; for example, only 17 per cent of housing authorities (less in the shires) would accept a woman's word that she had experienced violence at home, and social workers were most likely to be asked for verification (Evans & Duncan, 1988, pp.18–19). 'Prevention' in this context merely means delay and women who have been subject to violence and sent home again for reconciliation reappear with 'depressing frequency . . . often several times' (Niner, 1989, p. 42).

This is a sensitive issue for social workers, as we discussed in chapter 3; some research has suggested that they are reluctant to intervene in violence between adults, or even to recognise it, unless children are at risk, because of an overriding concern to maintain the family unit. The social workers with homeless families whom we interviewed felt strongly that women should be given the benefit of any doubt and that they should not be forced to remain in a violent relationship through the action, or inaction, of a helping agency. Their concern was to keep children safely with their mothers, not to persuade women to continue living with violent men.

The meaning of 'prevention' understood by social services managers is associated with the duty to prevent reception into care under children's legislation. That was also given in explanation for the Social Services Inspectorate's interest in family homelessness; and by the London Boroughs Association in opposing any possible diminution of housing departments' responsibilities which:

> would not make the homeless disappear. The weakening of housing authorities' duties to homeless people would not mean that local government could absolve itself from any responsibility towards them . . . Social services authorities have responsibilities under the Child Care Act . . . but as social services departments do not have a housing stock of

their own, [it] would probably mean that children would have to be taken into care. (LBA, 1989, p. 59)

Lack of adequate housing is a recurring factor in the background of families who are referred to social services departments, as recent research has shown (for example, Bebbington & Miles, 1989; Gibbons, 1990; Packman *et al.*, 1986). 'Unsatisfactory home conditions' continued to be cited as a major reason for care admissions during the 1980s, although homelessness was recorded less frequently as the only reason in the course of the decade: from 1379 of those currently in care at the end of 1979 down to 420 at the end of 1987, with 163 new admissions during 1988. The Department of Health's explanation, repeated in various parliamentary answers, was that: 'A child may be taken into care for a number of reasons of which homelessness may be a contributory factor, although not identified as a specific cause in the statistics' (for example, House of Commons Debates, 5 May 1987, written answers col. 366).

It is unclear from the statistics whether the consistent downward trend in admission of children to care solely because of their parents' homelessness reflected changes in housing departments' willingness to provide temporary accommodation, or a decline in social workers' readiness to receive into care for that reason at a time when care admissions generally were declining, although less markedly (Timaeus, 1990). A select committee recommendation, to fund research on admission of children into care because of homelessness, was not implemented (House of Commons Social Services Committee, 1984).

An appeal court ruling, that the social services preventive duty took precedence over a housing department's interpretation of its responsibilities, related to an 'intentionally' homeless family being kept in B & B by social services with Section One money. Investigation of 'intentionality' is discretionary but a family which is considered to have contrived homelessness deliberately or by default loses any right to be housed and even to remain in temporary accommodation. The implications of this ruling being applied to such families in general, so concerned the government that plans were made to modify the preventive duty and frame it in general terms for the Children Act 1989, unrelated to the needs of individual children in particular circumstances (DHSS, 1985, ch. 5). Moreover a new housing duty to co-operate with social services is qualified by what has been described as a 'designer loophole': applying only when compatible with the housing department's other duties and if it 'does not unduly prejudice the discharge of any of their functions' (S27). It seems that in the Children Act the government has tried to keep a distance between social work and housing activities and to minimise the potential for conflict over specific families.

Families who are judged to be 'intentionally' homeless have few options left and are likely to need continuing support over a long period to sustain them in difficult conditions. They may book themselves into B & B, if housing benefit will cover the bill; or squat; or move around staying with a series of relatives. If there is concern for the children, it can be quite an effort just keeping track of the family and ensuring that they get schooling and health checks. There is risk in losing such a family: Tyra Henry's mother was regarded as 'intentionally' homeless after 'abandoning' a tenancy and moving into her own mother's crowded flat. The housing department's refusal to rehouse the extended family together was identified by the inquiry panel as an important factor leading to renewed contact with the child's violent father and her subsequent death (Sedley, 1987).

Social workers and housing workers follow different interpretations of prevention. Social workers' idea of prevention would mean trying to get families accepted as statutorily homeless so that they remained safely together and did not become literally roofless, without anywhere to stay. Housing workers tend to see prevention in terms of minimising the number of successful applications. This can amount to denial and using all manner of delaying tactics in the hope that applicants will 'disappear'. A DoE survey found that the standard form of 'advice and assistance' offered as 'prevention' by 86 per cent of housing departments was useless lists of B & B hotels (Evans & Duncan, 1988, p. 29; Niner, 1989, pp. 27, 37, 40–1; Audit Commission, 1989A, para. 89). Regrettably these lists are often used by social services and probation as well. It is worse than useless to hand out misleading information to homeless people, so establishments should be visited and details regularly updated. This is a job which clients are able, and often willing, to do, especially if you can find some means of paying them.

The methods most commonly used by social workers are negotiation, particularly with the HPU, and advocacy directed at getting clients accepted as homeless. Families often approach social work agencies for this form of help, as surveys in temporary accommodation have shown. From the evidence available, between a quarter and a third of households accepted as homeless have had contact with a social worker before or at the time of leaving their last accommodation. They are most likely to be lone parents or pregnant single women, rather than couples with children; and up to three-quarters of women in refuges have contacted a social worker by the time of their last violent attack (Thomas & Niner, 1989, p. 75; Randall *et al.*, 1982, p. 26; Smith, 1989, p. 75).

In view of their opposing roles, it is not surprising when social workers are described as a problem for housing workers, making unwelcome referrals and allegedly taking insufficient account of the pressures on HPU staff. The Audit Commission (1989A, para. 84) reported that: 'Every housing department visited had experienced difficulties over referrals from social services... Housing officers thought that other agencies did not appreciate the difficulty of providing appropriate housing at short notice'. A report on local practices in Kent referred to:

> unrealistic expectations on both sides. The Housing Managers' perception of the problem is that the Social Services Department don't want to know and the Department's view of the Housing Managers is that they are taking a hard line which will force the break up of families. Homeless families (and especially Intentionally Homeless) become the focus of the accumulated irritations which build up between the two agencies. (Kent, 1981, paras 6.1–3)

Typically these issues and tensions apply to duty social work in area teams, or when crises arise in work with allocated child care cases.

On the other hand, the clients of specialist teams tend to be already inside the homelessness process, beyond the initial application stage. There the problem is likely to be how to reach families who have been rejected by the HPU, or are uncertain about applying. A social work team outposted in the housing department, as some are, is effectively dependent on it for referrals. They may be too closely identified with 'the system' to be acceptable to potential clients when they try to advertise their services as advocates. There are probably more drawbacks than advantages to outposting. However specialist homeless family social workers who are based in the SSD report a different problem: they may be expected to channel referrals from the rest of the department, which is the Audit Commission's recommended solution to bombardment on HPUs (1989A, para. 85). This can amount to inappropriate gate-keeping for another agency, likely to cause resentment among area team colleagues and also to de-skill those who no longer have to do their own negotiating.

Temporary accommodation

Although the Codes of Guidance make only a passing mention of social services involvement with families living in temporary accommodation, that is how the specialist social workers spend most of their time. The likelihood of a homeless family being placed in temporary accommodation, whilst awaiting rehousing, increased nearly eightfold during the 1980s to 37 900 households at the end of 1989, nearly a third of them in B & B hotels.

The different types of temporary accommodation include: 'short life' housing of various kinds, used by nearly a third of authorities; local authority hostels, used by half of all authorities, mainly metropolitan districts; and B & B hotels, used by two-thirds of authorities concentrated in London and some shire county districts. Two-fifths of all authorities, including nearly three-quarters of London boroughs, regularly use temporary accommodation outside their boundaries, mainly B & B (Evans & Duncan, 1988, pp. 3, 32).

B & B is reported to be the least popular type of temporary accommodation, among families placed there, on practically all accounts, although the other types may be little better. For example, hostels share with B & B many of the problems regarding access to services; warden supervision can be experienced as surveillance; and some families resent the stigma of being mixed with 'vulnerable' single homeless people who have been discharged from mental hospitals (Niner, 1989, ch. 3). 'Short life' housing awaiting refurbishment or demolition is often in a very poor physical condition.

On the other hand some families may be reluctant to move, for a variety of reasons: at least the rent and fuel bills are paid for them in hotels, whereas mounting debt is a likelihood after rehousing; friendships and communal support would be lost; the permanent tenancies on offer are in even worse condition or in 'bad' areas where lone mothers are afraid to take their children (a point also made by Bonnerjea & Lawton, 1987, pp. 46–7). This is a theme to which we shall return in chapter 5.

The main areas of difficulty for families in temporary accommodation have been identified as: first, access to mainstream services particularly education, health services and social security benefits; and secondly, personal health and safety. Educationists are concerned about children's interrupted or non-existent schooling and poor performance (ILEA, 1987A, B; HMI, 1990; similarly in the USA, Whitman *et al.*, 1990). If access problems could be solved Paul Corrigan, who was deputy director of the ILEA's education welfare service, envisaged a key role for schooling as a universal service: 'providing a bedrock for children and families experiencing the shifting and alienating experience of homelessness' (in SSI, 1989B, p. 30). However, a new specialist team of education welfare officers working in central London hotels was to be disbanded only three years later when the ILEA was abolished.

Health concerns have centred on: the poor diet of children living in B & B with inadequate cooking facilities, whose mothers therefore rely on take-away food; increased risk of infection in such crowded conditions; and difficulty in registering with GPs or being contacted by a health visitor, leading to over-use of hospital casualty facilities by homeless families (Conway, 1988; Health Visitors' Association & BMA, 1988; Association of Community Health Councils for England & Wales, 1989). Experimental specialist health services have not been entirely successful in locating their target population (for example, Lovell, 1986).

The health and education of children in temporary accommodation are underlying concerns for the responsible state agencies as much as the parents. Immediate problems with which families themselves seek help are more likely to be associated with money, particularly delay in social security benefits. Benefit delay is endemic in the social security system, affecting possibly a third of Income Support claimants, and it commonly follows a change of address, so homeless people are affected more than others (MORI, 1990, p. 15; Stewart & Stewart, 1991, ch. 3). Methods of organising advice sessions are discussed below.

Other issues which are important to families relate to personal safety. These include the dangers of confining young children to crowded and badly maintained buildings where there is unprotected electrical equipment, and an undercurrent of sexual and racial harassment, sometimes inflicted by hotel staff or other residents. Again there are predisposing factors: young lone mothers, who are vulnerable to sexual harassment, are also most likely to be placed in B & B (often in 'red light' districts), rather than in another, safer type of temporary accommodation (Niner, 1989). There is some evidence that racial minority families receive systematically worse treatment under homelessness procedures and are likely to spend longer in temporary accommodation (for example CRE, 1988; Bonnerjea & Lawton, 1987). Mutual aid probably offers the best protection against harassment and social workers can take the lead in forming a self help group. Experience indicates that there must be a relevant and neutral focus for such an initiative to be acceptable: 'keep fit' classes with a self-defence angle are a possibility that has worked.

Social work with families in temporary accommodation can best be understood in terms of mainstream social work with families and children. Its focus has to be practical and supportive:

The families tend to see their needs mainly in practical terms – housing, moving, money and furniture. Their overwhelming need is for reassurance about their housing position – will they be given permanent housing, how long will they have to wait, where will it be? The social work team feels strongly that these issues should be dealt with by the housing department, but the need is not recognised... Therefore the social workers spend a great deal of their time in temporary accommodation containing families' anxieties.

As one team leader explained:

The reason I would say that we as social workers need to be involved is largely from the advocacy point of view. So many of them feel so dependent on the state systems whether it's for money or for housing, and just feel that they can't fight for that on their own . . . It doesn't necessarily have to be social workers, but I mean it is one of the social work functions.

It is useful to experiment with different ways of contacting families. Being notified of new arrivals by the HPU or by hostel/hotel managers can be unsatisfactory for two reasons: it is unreliable; and families at this stage in the homelessness process may find it intrusive to be approached by a social worker. Holding 'surgeries' at regular times which are publicly advertised has the advantage of leaving the initiative with families, and also of being accessible to others who have referred themselves to B & B but whose circumstances are very much the same as those who are statutorily homeless. Getting co-operation from the hotel management is rarely a problem because the availability of advice takes pressure off their own staff.

However duty social workers can soon become overwhelmed with repetitive requests for routine information about, for example, the whereabouts of local schools and the social security office. Information leaflets can reduce bombardment and lower families' anxiety levels. Social workers are then able to concentrate on queries which require their negotiating skills and sensitive handling, such as complaints about conditions in the hotel which are difficult because likely to bring workers into conflict with the hotel management. Similarly requests for transfer to better temporary accommodation are not welcomed by HPU staff but support from a social worker makes a move more likely (Thomas & Niner, 1989, p. 16).

An obvious response to the dearth of facilities for families in temporary accommodation is to set up new ones. Day care and play space are priorities in a situation where more under-fives may be concentrated than in all of an authority's children's homes combined. Sometimes a room for this purpose can be negotiated within a large hotel, but more often local premises would have to be found where mothers could bring their children from surrounding hotels: a church hall, perhaps. Drop-in centres for families living in temporary accommodation are specifically recommended in Department of Health guidance on the Children Act (DoH, 1991A, para. 3.16).

Child protection

Counselling about relationships and child care difficulties is valued by many families, because of the stresses involved in going through the homelessness process; although families may need encouragement to ask for help. Reactive counselling and support can shade into more pro-active child protection, of which families may be suspicious and openly hostile. The London directors' Code of Practice shows that they were worried about the possibility of a child abuse death in temporary accommodation (ADSS, 1985).

So far, there has been no child abuse fatality resulting in an inquiry report while a family was actually living in temporary accommodation, although at least six deaths in the mid/late 1980s have been the children of formerly home-less families. Tyra Henry's mother has already been mentioned as 'intentionally' homeless. Stephanie Fox's parents were placed in a residential family centre before being housed under homelessness procedures in a high-rise flat as their first home (that case is discussed further in chapter 5). The mothers of Sukina Hammond and Liam Johnson took refuge in temporary accommodation from their partner's violence but returned because there seemed to be no alternative. The mothers of Kimberley Carlile and Doreen Mason met and moved in with violent partners while they were homeless (Sedley, 1987; Wandsworth, 1990; Avon, 1989; Islington, 1989; Blom Cooper, 1987; Southwark, 1989).

There appears to be more professional anxiety than actual risk of serious abuse in temporary accommodation (as we argue in Stewart & Stewart, 1992A), but it is also clear that homeless mothers and their children are especially vulnerable to violent men. The absence of men in hotels crowded with lone mothers, and the knowledge that one can easily be overheard, as the partition walls have no sound proofing, are probably the main reasons for the relative lack of violence. Neglect is the problem more commonly reported by health visitors, hotel staff, and other residents: parents who do not feed their children, leave them in wet and soiled clothes, do not supervise them adequately and leave them alone for hours.

The Department of Health's guide to assessing the need for child protection offers no guidance for social workers on how to assess 'reasonable parenting' in the highly abnormal environment of a B & B hotel; it is generally defined as what a reasonable person would do in a given situation. While recognising the strains associated with 'poor housing' – homelessness is not mentioned – the Orange Book warns: 'Nevertheless, parents have a responsibility to provide adequate shelter, clothing, warmth and food for their children' (DoH, 1988, p. 63). This is both unfair and unrealistic. When assessing the risk to a child in temporary accommodation, social workers should be careful not to blame the parents for their situation, and not to penalise them for being homeless.

Inter-agency relations

The Audit Commission (1989A, pp.32,52) called for improved liaison procedures between housing and social services departments, and the Code of Guidance has emphasised this as 'vital' (DoE *et al.*, 1991B, para. 15.4). Specialist homeless families social work teams and their housing counterparts have necessarily developed collaborative arrangements (as argued by senior social worker Owens, 1988). But co-operation with housing departments is not generally a priority for social services management; they are not, for example, included in the revised guidelines for working with other agencies over child protection (DoH, 1991C). With the exception of young people leaving care, the Children Act guidance does not give priority to co-operation with housing departments, which is comparable to the NHS and Community Care Act guidance relating to the adult client groups (discussed in chapter 2).

Similarly housing departments tend to work independently of other services, seeking 'co-operation' only when they want something done. Hence social workers giving evidence to the Tyra Henry inquiry regarded their housing department 'like the weather', unpredictable and impervious to influence (Sedley, 1987, pp. 44–5). Many social services departments have someone at middle management level designated to liaise with housing (more feasible in single-tier authorities than in shire counties where there are several housing departments to each SSD). This can be useful on policy issues, and is effectively a requirement in planning provision for care leavers and discharged mental hospital patients. But liaison at management level is relevant to practitioners only if an impasse has been reached in negotiations about a particular case and you want to go 'over the head' of another housing worker in the Homeless Persons Unit, for example. It is possible for formal liaison procedures actually to impede co-operation, if they are remote and insensitive to the needs of practitioners.

Agency setting is important in providing a balance between closeness and distance which is necessary for constructive collaboration at practitioner level. So sharing office premises can be useful when the territory is neutral and independent of either department; for example, a converted flat on an estate where formerly homeless families are housed. Social workers and housing officers are the most likely groups to share premises in the decentralised, neighbourhood teams which were established in several authorities during the 1980s (we discuss neighbourhood working in chapter 5).

Seconding or outposting of social workers into the housing department's HPU is generally not effective, although it has been favoured by the Audit Commission (1989A, para. 85) and the Association of District Councils (1987). It tends to lead either to conflict and isolation or, more commonly, incorporation into the attitudes and working practices of the dominant host agency, to the detriment of good social work practice. The most reliable prospect for successful collaboration would combine separate agency location, with negotiated liaison procedures, and a clear professional identity for both groups. That entails specialist homeless families teams retaining a generic social work role, with responsibility for any child care or mental health statutory work. The teams which appear to have the least satisfactory relationships with their own departments are those where statutory work has to be referred on; by implication they are not 'real' social workers.

Besides inter-professional, inter-departmental and inter-agency relations, there is an inter-authority dimension in conurbations where homeless families are commonly placed far from their local neighbourhood. As already noted, two-fifths of all authorities, including nearly three-quarters of London boroughs, regularly use temporary accommodation outside their own boundaries. Disruption to family life and difficulties for local services are both amplified in this situation, imposing pressures on clients and on practitioners in the receiving area, who can offer only inadequate help. In response to that situation, some boroughs have appointed outreach social workers to visit vulnerable families already known to the department who have been placed in temporary accommodation elsewhere. This is preferable to the alternative of having to transfer supervision every time a family is moved, and possibly losing contact altogether – although it remains official policy that services must be provided by the authority where a family is, not where they came from.

Conclusion

Social work with homeless families became more necessary
during the 1980s as increasing numbers of young families had
to spend longer periods of time going through the homelessness process. These developments found practitioners and
their managers trying to reconcile policy makers' expectations
about what social workers should do, with the continuing
needs of clients whose circumstances saw little or no improvement. In the housing stress areas of inner cities, where
statutory homelessness procedures have become the standard
route into a council tenancy, the stress of living in temporary
accommodation has to be endured as the price of getting
rehoused. However in the next chapter we shall consider how
living on council estates generates its own problems which
social services and probation need to address.

Note

1. We do not consider the legal and administrative details of statutory
   homelessness. There are plenty of guides and manuals named in the
   Resource List: for example, Arden (1986A & 1986B; the first is
   legalistic and the second for applicants themselves); Dowell (1989)
   is for skilled advisers; Randall *et al.* (1989) for the general user;
   Watchman & Robson (1989) is a well-respected guide for the more
   experienced adviser. All the guides and manuals referred to in
   chapter 3, on relationship breakdown as it affects women, deal with
   homelessness. Most of the guides for young people leaving home or
   care consider the various, most often non-statutory, help they may
   seek if homeless (see chapter 2, note 1).

5

Difficult Estates

In every city and most towns there is at least one housing estate where few people live, or even visit, unless they have to. These are sometimes called 'problem estates', and they are said to be inhabited by 'problem families'. 'Difficult' is a less perjorative description which still conveys how such estates are regarded by housing managers and tenants alike. In this chapter we shall discuss how estates become difficult; what it is like living there; why they are of particular concern to social workers and probation officers; and how working practices have developed in response to clients impoverished quality of life.

Difficult-to-let

From the local housing department's point of view, tenancies on some estates are always difficult-to-let, meaning that they present management problems and are an unreliable source of rent income. This is recognised by the DoE in central government, which keeps a national list of difficult estates and, over the decades, has introduced a series of policies designed to tackle the situation. How can it be that the worst estates become almost unlettable, while so many people remain homeless?

Explanations

According to Oscar Wilde's account of men's rise to fame and fortune some are born great, some achieve greatness and some have greatness thrust upon them. Reverse, negative processes are apparent in the creation of difficult estates: some are badly built, by design or construction; some start well but fall into disrepair; and some are used as 'sinks' in discriminatory allocation policies.

Any design fault is amplified by the scale of a modern mass housing estate. The overall impact can be so intimidating that a homeless refugee mother was moved to take high court action to avoid being housed on the Chalkhill Estate in Brent, because it reminded her of prisons where she had been incarcerated in her country of origin (*Times Law Report*, 13 May 1991). Design details acquire disproportionate significance: inappropriately positioned access decks can become wind tunnels; concrete extension balconies act as bridges, conducting the cold from outside straight into people's living rooms; uninsulated picture windows are ill-suited to the British climate, letting expensive central heating out to warm the sky. High density developments on cheap in-fill sites are sometimes unsuitable locations for residential use. An example would be a tower block built between a main road and a railway line which would become a trap of atmospheric and noise pollution with no safe place for children to play. On the other hand, the vast estates spread in remote places on the outskirts of conurbations often lack any public amenities, with residents also isolated from work opportunities.

Some of the building materials and methods used in the construction of mass housing have created problems for future tenants. Experimental use of pre-fabricated concrete slabs produced cold, damp buildings which were prone to condensation and mould growth, and hard to heat. Ducts and void spaces behind the panels provide an environment for all kinds of vermin to live and move around unimpeded. Cost-cutting by skimping on safety standards and the quality of materials left some buildings structurally unsound. Dunleavy (1981) tells how the political influence of big construction firms in the 1950s led local authorities to demolish old housing and build high-rise estates, which became more of a liability than an asset with many having been expensively demolished.

While it is probably now the case that most difficult-to-let tenancies are on high- or medium-rise estates, the 'problem estate' as traditionally presented consists of ordinary houses with gardens, built for slum clearance during the inter-war period. Life on two such estates is discussed, very differently from Marxist and pluralist perspectives, by Damer (1989) and Reynolds (1986). Typically an estate whose residents were stigmatised by having come from the 'slums', would be allowed by the council landlord to fall into disrepair. Whether or not the houses were well built originally, neglect and heavy use by generations of children would take their toll. Any opportunity would be taken to seek a transfer off the estate, and tenancies would be relet to people who could get nothing better.

By whichever process an estate becomes undesirable to live in and therefore difficult-to-let, allocation policy can have the effect of reinforcing its bad reputation. If tenancy offers are made in a way which effectively cannot be refused by applicants who have no choice, a situation is soon reached whereby most residents do not want to live there. That happened originally to many old estates which were built for slum clearance.

More recently, statutory homelessness procedures have become the standard route on to difficult estates. A DoE survey found that three-quarters of local authorities make only one offer of rehousing to families who have been homeless (Evans & Duncan, 1988, p. 3). Commonly these would be tenancies which could not otherwise be let. Four years before the famous 'riot' took place on Broadwater Farm estate in Haringey, the local social work area team reported that 85 per cent of available tenancies were being let to formerly homeless people and that this contributed to low morale and a 'siege mentality' on the estate (*Social Work Today*, 15 February 1983, p. 8).

It can be particularly hard for families who have endured the stress of homelessness to be allocated to an unfamiliar but possibly notorious estate miles away from their home area. There is a suspicion that some housing departments use this prospect as a threat to deter potential homeless applicants. A senior social worker told us it had been described to her by housing colleagues as a: 'locational disincentive – families are rehoused in areas where they do not want to live to deter others from using the homelessness route to rehousing'. Huge peripheral estates attached to the outer suburbs of cities – such as Easterhouse in Glasgow and Netherley outside Liverpool – have become the most chronically 'difficult estates' for tenants and housing managers alike (Maclennan *et al.*, 1990). Inner city problems attract political attention, perhaps because they are more visible, while the outer estates remain neglected.

The changing character of 'difficult' estates is associated with a trend which has been described as the residualisation of council housing (for example, by Forrest & Murie, 1988). During the 1980s a virtual end to new building, combined with tenants' right to buy their homes at a discount, caused contraction in the public sector at a time when demand for affordable rented housing was increasing because of rising unemployment. The dwindling supply of what is now called 'social' housing (to differentiate it from the open market in property) became concentrated in the large and less desirable estates, where no-one wanted to buy. Reduced maintenance budgets meant that disrepair was slow to be remedied and living conditions on these estates deteriorated further.

Rents, however, were increased to such an extent, under central government instruction, that 60 per cent of council tenants nationally were entitled to means tested housing benefit, so that they could pay the rent. Thus it became apparent that local authority housing was 'reserved for the poor', as Cullingworth had anticipated (CHAC, 1969, p. 21). A fashionable explanation for this trend is that a new 'underclass' has emerged, composed largely of council tenants living on run-down estates and dependent on a 'benefit culture'. The very existence of so many poor people concentrated together is said to represent a threat to social order (Murray, 1990). 'Underclass' is not a new concept, as Macnicol (1987) has demonstrated, originating in eugenicist writing about 'problem families' during the inter-war period; but once revived it was well-received in the repressive political climate of the 1980s.

Policy responses

Central and local government policies for dealing with difficult estates have varied over the decades from improvement, through demolition and redevelopment, to privatisation, or decentralisation. It is fair to say that none of these approaches has been entirely satisfactory from anyone's point of view, although some have been more successful than others.

Policies for improving run-down housing were concentrated on the private rented sector in inner cities during the 1960s and 1970s, with special funding for 'area treatment' programmes such as General Improvement Areas and Housing Action Areas. As it became apparent during the 1980s that some of the worst repaired housing was in the public sector, the reaction from central government was to blame local authorities. A series of reports by the Audit Commission (notably 1986A & B) criticised council landlords – particularly Labour-controlled London boroughs – for inefficiency over rent collection, estate maintenance and control of empty property. From the local authority side it was pointed out that budgets for housing management had been cut and councils were not even allowed to use their capital receipts from enforced sales.

Mistrust and 'friction' between central and local government were soon identified as important factors affecting the implementation of policies to improve urban areas, including the new Estate Action Initiative. The other main handicap was an inadequate level of funding to meet the scale of the disrepair problem, which was estimated to require £900 million a year (Audit Commission, 1989B; Pinto, 1991). Some estates were structurally so unsound that improvement was not viable and demolition became the only realistic option, but even that could cost more money than was available.

Privatisation was central government's real agenda and their preferred mechanism for applying it to difficult estates was through the formation of Housing Action Trusts (HATs). The government's ability to designate potential HAT estates without consultation, and the peculiar form of democracy which was allowed for 'tenants' choice' – whereby abstentions and non-voters counted in *favour* of a change in ownership – presented a challenge for community work, which enjoyed something of a revival. Local campaigns to mobilise tenant opinion produced widespread support for remaining with local authority landlords rather than joining the private sector, and the HAT programme collapsed (Woodward, 1991; Rao, 1990; Fraser, 1988, is a practical guide for tenant groups: see Resource List). Subsequently a few Labour councils recaptured some initiative when the DoE agreed to adapt the HAT formula and divert unused funds to finance estate improvements which would be under local control (Black, 1991; DoE, 1990A).

The alternative stratagem which was favoured by local authority and professional housing representatives – to tackle acknowledged shortcomings whilst avoiding an increasingly residual role for the public sector – involved decentralising estate management and promoting tenant participation (ALA, 1987; IoH, 1987; Bartram, n.d.). As such it selectively supported that aspect of government policy which was associated with the popular but small-scale Priority Estates Project, established and publicised by Anne Power, who formerly worked in a neighbourhood advice centre in Islington (Power, 1987; 1991). There is no clear evidence that a decentralised repair service of itself necessarily gets the work done any more effectively, although it is more attractive to community workers and local activists (Pilkington & Kendrick, 1987).

A negative impression is conveyed in much of the research demostrating that difficult estates are part of a government housing policy to provide public housing on a mass scale and that it was fatally flawed in the first place. One such critic is Coleman (1985) who proposes various remedial measures to do with security and access. Others are yet more negative: these estates are irredeemable and, when it comes to policies for improvement, 'nothing works'. Thus a report on Sheffield's 2700-flatted Hyde Park estate concluded that: 'Some problems simply cannot be overcome as long as the estate remains standing'. But observing from the outside, as a non-housing sociologist, Rock (in Hope & Shaw, 1988) concludes that on the contrary 'anything works': estate residents are so marginalised and neglected that almost any kind of attention by people in authority has the effect of improving their morale and quality of life.

Difficult to live in

Three main areas of difficulty stand out in accounts of life on the worst estates: debt, ill health and concerns about personal safety. We shall examine each in turn.

Debt

Serious debt is commonly linked to poverty, but that is not always the case. Most people in the general population who get into debt have fallen behind with commercial credit agreements (Berthoud & Kempson, 1990). While credit card or hire purchase debts may be associated with a reduction or interruption of income, the people concerned would not necessarily regard themselves as poor in other respects. Arrears of commercial credit should be distinguished from inability to pay essential bills, for housing and fuel in particular, where the potential consequences are much more serious and most likely to affect people on the lowest benefit income (Ford, 1991). Of course many people get into multiple debt, when they have to try and balance one creditor against another. In that situation, more demanding commercial creditors are likely to be given precedence over those regular, essential bills which should take priority for the sake of housing security and a continuing fuel supply. Various handbooks are available for use in advising people who are in debt; and there are specialist money advice centres in many areas to which social workers can refer clients.[1] This is particularly useful as debt counselling is a time-consuming business; however you should refer someone to another agency only if you are sure that this is acceptable to them, otherwise they may not go and will therefore not get the help they need.

Fuel bills can be unusually high in badly insulated concrete buildings where there is constant heat loss; and tenants who complain about condensation and mould growth are often unhelpfully advised to turn up the heating and open a window. These extra costs used to be recognised in social security policy, with weekly additions to benefit for claimants living on 'hard to heat' estates, but all such allowances for 'additional requirements' were abolished in 1988. So with nothing to compensate tenants for the disproportionate expense of living on difficult estates, fuel debt is common.

Similarly rent arrears are more likely than average, particularly on modern high-rise estates where rents are high. Some components of the rent are not eligible for rebate through housing benefit, such as charges for district central heating systems which cover the whole estate and are often not under the control of individual tenants. 'Ineligible rent' has to be made up from the tenant's income support, with no extra allowance. Housing benefit entitlement covers the claimant, partner and dependent children; anyone else living with them, such as a grandparent or grown-up sons and daughters, is regarded as an independent 'assessment unit' and a standard 'non-dependent deduction' is made from the tenant's housing benefit whether or not these relatives make any contribution to paying the rent. On outer estates where practically all the young people are unemployed and many are disqualified from claiming income support (being under 18), their families easily build up rent arrears because of the 'non-dependent' rule.[2]

Most councils are reluctant to evict tenants who are in arrears with the rent, particularly if they would have an obligation to rehouse the family under homeless persons legislation (see chapter 4). Some use bailiffs to seize household goods which are auctioned at knock-down prices to cancel the debt: a more common practice with poll tax arrears. The most likely outcome is that repayments of rent arrears will be deducted at source by the DSS from the tenant's income support, thereby reducing their disposable income and therefore their capacity to deal with other debts. 'Fuel direct' is also a popular solution with the electricity and gas boards, but the trend under the privatised utilities is towards installing power card meters which can be pre-calibrated to recover arrears at the same time as charging for current consumption. However little fuel the consumer uses, if the meter is not fed to reduce arrears, the supply cuts off: a simple form of self-inflicted disconnection, which has the added advantage for the supplier of being concealed from official scrutiny and any associated publicity.

Ill health

Inter-connections between poverty, ill health and bad housing are complex, enduring and hard to prove; some of the main aspects are discussed in chapter 6. The British Medical Association (1987) identified four processes by which deprivation affects health: physiological, psychological, behavioural and professional. Stated simply this means that people, particularly children, who are poor and badly housed are under-nourished, suffer from cold related illnesses and are prone to chronic sickness. Their mothers experience psychological stress and are likely to develop unhealthy habits such as smoking. People living in the worst areas have the least access to health services. Nor do they start from an equal base: adults and children with disabilities are much more likely than the general population to live in council housing because they have lower income and higher expenses, therefore less choice (Cooke & Lawton, 1985). They also tend to get the worst tenancies on estates – on upper floors rather than at ground level, for example (Littlewood & Tinker, 1981).

Whenever health risk is used as an argument for enforcing improvements in the worst housing, the complainants are expected to produce evidence. This has resulted, over the years, in various attempts by researchers and others to prove the obvious: namely, that living on difficult estates is bad for you. Thus Byrne *et al.* (1985 & 1986) in Gateshead and a Scottish team of researchers (Martin, 1989; Platt *et al.*, 1989) set out to make the case for tenants' groups on difficult estates, resulting in convincing research reports but no consequent action from the housing authorities concerned. Holman (1988), writing from Easterhouse estate in Glasgow, has argued that tenants should conduct such research themselves, and that also has been tried. A tenants' group in a Birmingham tower block persuaded a local magistrate that the council should be required to repair the whole estate, which was affected by condensation and mould growth, but the judgement was overturned on appeal. The city council successfully argued that each tenant on the estate must separately prove that the condition of her/his flat constituted a health hazard and a 'statutory nuisance' (*Times Law Report*, 25 June 1987). The collective case for improvement was fragmented and lost.

Safety

A constant atmosphere of aggravation is reported from difficult estates. Racial and sexual harassment and frequent exposure to crime on the one hand, and aggressive policing on the other, erodes the quality of life and makes people feel insecure. A study in Brent found that background aggravation was as much feared as domestic violence, and as likely to be a cause of homelessness (Bonnerjea & Lawton, 1987, ch. 4). Reflecting these concerns a Scottish judge ruled that a teenage girl would be more 'at risk' in her own flat on a difficult estate than she already was sleeping in a tent, and instructed the social work department to place her with an approved landlady, thereby relieving the housing department of responsibility towards her (Kelly v. Monklands District Council).

Regrettably some measures to restore safety have had the effect of introducing a further element of perceived injustice. Thus a new public order offence of 'disorderly conduct', which was intended for use against 'hooligans on housing estates' who made old people afraid by 'throwing things down the stairs, banging on doors, peering in at windows, and knocking over dustbins', was seen as a further means of police oppressing youth for doing nothing specifically illegal (Home Office, 1985). How to deal with racial harassment, both effectively and fairly, became a major issue once the existence of the problem was recognised. The common response of housing departments was to offer a transfer off the estate to minority victims, leaving the racist perpetrators of harassment undisturbed, which was clearly unfair. It became the policy of both the CRE (1987) and the AMA

(1985) that harassers should be evicted and victims protected in their existing homes (also see Resource List: Forbes, 1988 on legal remedies). However getting police action and a conviction to support eviction, is difficult. The House of Commons Home Affairs Committee (1986) suggested that social workers were best placed to mediate and sort everything out without trouble – which was resisted by the AMA as another unwelcome imposition of an impossible task.

Racial conflict and aggressive policing were recurrent features of the 'riots' reported from English inner cities during the first half of the 1980s, several of which occurred on difficult estates, notably Broadwater Farm in the north London borough of Haringey. Twenty large, flatted estates in London were regarded by the Metropolitan Police as likely locations of further 'riots' (*Guardian*, 12 July 1986, p. 2). The very existence of such concentrations of working class housing was presented as a 'law and order' issue, the Broadwater Farm estate in particular being described as a criminal 'rookery'. The inquiry commissioned by Haringey council concluded that the estate had a 'terrible image' (Gifford, 1986). All this was symptomatic of what has been described as the criminalisation of social policies during the Thatcher decade, whereby the significance of social problems was guaged by their perceived threat to public order. Policies towards difficult housing estates would be construed and justified in terms of crime prevention (an approach implicitly followed by Home Office researchers Hope & Shaw, 1988).

Attitudes to crime tend to be polarised, and policies which essentially treat residents as offenders (which many may be) are unlikely to be responsive to their needs as victims (which they may also be). Thus women's and black tenant groups report difficulty in getting their views listened to by agencies which are primarily concerned with keeping order (for example, Ware, 1988, p. 5; Limehouse, 1987). Police reluctance to take action over offences committed against, rather than by, residents of difficult estates tends to result in low confidence and under-reporting (discussed by Gifford, 1986). Alternative forms of protection are based on containment through engineered neighbourliness. Projects run by NACRO's Safe Neighbourhood Unit promote a version of suburban Neighbourhood Watch for inner city tenants. Local conciliation and mediation schemes between warring residents have been established on estates in, for example, Birmingham and the east London borough of Newham. While high claims are sometimes made for the effectiveness of such initiatives, their scale is only small in relation to the hundreds of thousands of people who live on the country's difficult estates.

Social work concerns

The main reason for social work concern about difficult estates is that so many clients live on them. A high proportion of referrals to both social services departments and the probation service come from areas of council housing and this can be seen throughout the country, including southern shire counties where the public housing sector is very small in comparison with other tenures. Systematic evidence for this is scarce beyond the level of individual authorities, but two national surveys covering 21 SSDs and 17 probation areas found 62 per cent and 41 per cent of clients respectively were council tenants (compared with 21 per cent of housing stock nationally). Most of the rest, being without independent accommodation, were therefore formally tenureless although many who lived with relatives (11 per cent of SSD clients, 23 per cent probation) would actually have been in council housing (Stewart & Stewart, 1991, p. 17).

Of course not all of these referrals come from difficult estates, but local evidence suggests that many do and ordinary estates often contain some of the same problematic features, from the residents' point of view. Child care referrals, in particular, tend to be concentrated in the worst housing: this was a finding of research in SSDs during the 1970s and 1980s (for example, Goldberg & Warburton, 1979; Packman, 1986). Those were mainly voluntary child care cases (by Packman's classification) but another study found that the parents of children whom social workers regarded as being seriously 'at risk', tended to be more dissatisfied with their housing than other families referred from the same neighbourhood (Gibbons, 1990).

Trying to establish linkages between housing conditions, or any other manifestations of poverty, and child abuse is a problematic business, fraught with empirical and ideological pitfalls (some of which are discussed by Parton in Violence Against Children Study Group, 1990). Obviously most parents who are badly housed do not harm their children, but equally, the constraints imposed by housing conditions, and the structural context of housing deprivation, form the backdrop to so much child protection work that they cannot be discounted. Certain factors recur in research reports: sleep loss and intolerance of babies crying in crowded buildings with poor sound insulation, was highlighted by Thoburn (1980). Difficulties in disciplining children and harsh restraint in unsafe play were associated with overcrowded housing and lack of private space, by Wilson and Herbert (1978). The researchers and parents alike attributed unsatisfactory child rearing practices to the environmental constraints under which the families were living. Similarly, Home Office researchers linked early onset of delinquency with parents' inability to supervise play in and near crowded homes without neighbourhood facilities (Riley & Shaw, 1985).

The connections are evident between housing circumstances and difficulties in bringing up children, but any search for causal relationships with abuse is misguided, because it would isolate one factor, albeit an important one, in a family's experience at the expense of ignoring others of maybe greater importance. The oppressive influence of patriarchy on family relationships is one such over-riding factor, whilst another is the unreasonable expectations which are made of parents' ability to cope under almost any material adversity. The concept of 'reasonable parenting', which permeates the Children Act 1989, seems to set a variable standard of care, adjustable according to the family's living conditions. Objection could be sustained on grounds of social justice because the existence of acceptable levels of deprivation appears to be taken for granted; however one might at least expect that allowances would consequently be made. The Department of Health's guide to assessment acknowledges that 'poor housing can place considerable strains on families', but then stresses that nevertheless 'parents have a responsibility to provide adequate shelter . . . for their children', despite any 'environmental factors beyond their control', which they are evidently expected to overcome (DoH, 1988, p. 63). The conclusion must be that poor and badly housed parents have to try harder, but social workers must be aware of this and guard against appearing to penalise families.

Housing problems are a recurrent theme running through most of the child abuse inquiry reports about deaths which occurred during the 1980s. However, this is nowhere acknowledged, and as the DoH-commissioned review of the reports recognises, 'the effects of environmental disadvantage are not generally analysed' (Noyes, 1991, p.109). We have already observed in chapter 4 that many of those who died were the children of formerly homeless families and many of them had been rehoused on to difficult estates. In fact the details in some of these reports read like the DoE's catalogue of the nationally most 'difficult-to-let' estates: the Ferrier Estate in Greenwich, Aylesbury Estate in Southwark, Sholver Estate in the Pennines outside Oldham.

The report on the death of Doreen Mason gave a profile of the 2000-flatted Aylesbury Estate, where 'Normal conditions included high unemployment, high density population, poor housing conditions, a high and rising crime rate, drug abuse, poor take-up of health services, a high level of single parenthood, and high levels of child abuse. Primary prevention . . . was difficult to achieve'. The Ferrier Estate, where Kimberley Carlile died, was described in similar terms and the Commission of Inquiry commented 'we heard hardly a good word about the place', where 7000 people lived in 1900 homes. 'We were told that those who can, move off the Estate' and that 'the overwhelming majority of people who live on the Estate would rather live somewhere else'. However, 'Many worse estates are to be found across the country, so that the "survivors" in Ferrier are not even awarded the kudos that goes with bringing up a family successfully in, say, the East End of London'.

Greenwich council was credited with, 'Many attempts . . . to make the Ferrier Estate a decent place in which to live', whereas the housing policies of Wandsworth council were specifically said to have contributed to the death of Stephanie

Fox. Privatisation of more desirable estates in the borough had left the council with only 28 000 tenancies, mainly contained in 180 high rise blocks, and responsibility for housing 1000 homeless families a year. This meant that families with young children were necessarily being allocated flats high above the ground – on the 19th floor in the Fox case, despite social work attempts to get a 'more appropriate' offer. The Panel commented:

> We were surprised that such a young and vulnerable family were housed so high . . . Apart from all other considerations, it was not possible to get a triple buggy into the lift . . . The diminishing housing stock has clearly affected Council housing policy and we believe that the increased pressure on the family created by such accommodation played its part in increasing the risk to Stephanie. (Wandsworth, 1990)

What social workers do

Resettlement

Both the Fox and Carlile families had recently moved on to difficult estates after spending extended periods in homeless families' accommodation. Resettling newly housed, formerly homeless families and discharged mental hospital patients has long been regarded as an appropriate social work task (for example, Smith, 1966; Hooper *et al.*, 1978), although it becomes a low priority under pressure of other work, and the specialist resettlement teams rarely have enough time to follow clients through – that is, unless they have some strong ulterior motive: one such team we interviewed would offer six months' social work support and a rent guarantee as an incentive for the housing department to rehouse families who were regarded as 'intentionally' homeless and who would otherwise probably break up. The Scottish Code of Guidance actually expects social workers to undertake redemption of 'intentionally' homeless applicants – by modifying 'persistent anti-social behaviour' and starting to pay off arrears – before rehousing is considered (SDD, 1980, para. 2.21). This kind of pressure can be difficult to resist when housing departments control the resources.

Many housing officers consider that all relevant needs are met by the offer of a tenancy, and see no problem for a family moving on to a difficult estate in an unfamiliar area without support. Others recognise that 'remedying homelessness means more than providing an empty dwelling. A "home" is more than this', but generally lack time to do anything about it. DoE-commissioned researchers were told that some people were considered '"unrehousable" – that is, unable to sustain an orthodox council tenancy without guaranteed social work support', and that housing managers resented that such a guarantee was not usually forthcoming. A few housing departments employ their own resettlement workers and the researchers concluded, 'this reflects perceived diffi-culties in ensuring that social work support will always be available where needed' (Niner, 1989, pp. 77–8; Thomas & Niner, 1989, p. 21).

Seebohm would have approved. His committee recom-mended that:

> The full range of housing responsibilities should be placed upon housing departments. To relieve them of responsibil-ity for dependent or unreliable tenants would discourage them from looking at the housing needs of their area as a whole and create or reinforce degrading stigmas and social distinctions.

They suggested that to facilitate this, and where resources permitted, social services staff should be attached to housing departments, constituting 'a valuable preventive measure, particularly in large new housing estates', although as we noted in chapter 4 such outpostings may not work well in practice (Seebohm, 1968, paras 401, 413).

Where arrangements like this were made, they were seen as a form of community development. Most of the new towns, for example, had 'social development officers' who contacted new arrivals and responded to problems which might arise later from changing circumstances (Harloe & Horrocks, 1974; Else in Henderson *et al.*, 1980, ch.7). This practice continued until the new town development corporations were wound up and their housing sold or transferred to other landlords, by the late eighties. Among the last of the new towns, Warrington and Runcorn had a team of six social workers who did non-statutory work with tenants, and one of whom had specific responsibility for formerly homeless families.

Neighbourhood organisation

Generally any continuing work with families and individuals who are rehoused on difficult estates is now left to the social work agencies – local authority and probation – which already cover the area. Unfortunately these agencies are under so much pressure that they can scarcely accommodate the new work which is constantly being referred. The inquiry into the death of Doreen Mason accepted that her mother had not been allocated to a social worker when pregnant, although she was thought to have killed a previous child, because at that stage: 'the case could not be regarded as a high priority by comparison with the work being undertaken in (that Area of Lambeth) and the staff available to do the work'.

Decentralised organisation of social services to a neighbourhood 'patch' level, where social work could have a community focus, was a management response favoured during the 1980s. Community social work and neighbourhood organisation, in both SSDs and the probation service, was promoted from the National Institute for Social Work as being particularly applicable to teams under bombardment on difficult estates, because it encouraged a group approach rather than the traditional, individualistic form of social work. It could respond to local perceptions of need, thereby promising efficiency of scale which could be also supported on more principled grounds. This was thought to be consumerist and therefore more acceptable to local communities. Productivity and job satisfaction would be increased, as would inter-agency co-operation, particularly with housing departments, with which many decentralised teams shared offices. One of the main proponents, Barbara Hearn, had previously been team leader on a difficult estate in Lewisham (Hearn & Thomson, 1987; Henderson, 1986). Many authorities adopted neighbourhood organisation of social work services with some changing to entirely decentralised housing and social services.

However the neighbourhood reorganisation of social services was criticised by the Commission of Inquiry into the death of Kimberley Carlile, mainly for the extra demands which it placed on workers who were already under bombardment. The social work team covering the Ferrier Estate had recently been decentralised, and the report commented on 'how fragile isolated teams can be', recommending that: 'The workload of decentralised teams should be carefully reviewed to judge how far their very availability affects referrals, both in terms of number and in terms of how consistent their pattern is with the Department's priorities'. Overwork, rather than poor judgement or malpractice, was associated with that particular child's death. The danger, within a community social work approach, of neglecting isolated, uncooperative and stigmatised individuals in favour of more socially acceptable but less problematic clients, has been highlighted by other commentators (such as the practitioners who were interviewed by Henderson, 1986).

Further points were made by a social worker from the Broadwater Farm Estate team, after the 1985 riot. He wrote of the need to maintain a professional identity whilst practising community social work, otherwise the justification for being there would be lost. Being based on the estate and identifying with the residents carried its own risk: 'Given the political and social isolation of the community we serve, it is quite possible that our professional experience will be similarly marginalised and isolated from the mainstream of social work practice itself'. He questioned the viability of 'professional detachment' in these circumstances and concluded that: 'inevitably a degree of politicisation will take place which in turn will have to be applied to our professional practice . . . if we are not to become redundant and extinct' (Hutchinson-Reis, 1986). Similar issues were raised by social workers from an estate-based team in Nottingham (Dillon & Parker, 1988).

The possibility of alienation from the social-work-in-local-government mainstream, when teams on difficult estates take their work seriously, seems not to have concerned the advocates of decentralisation.

Negotiation

A common feature of social work on difficult estates is that the majority of clients are self-referred (an obvious consequence of local accessibility) and they generally bring queries of a practical nature arising from poverty and conditions on the estate. Teams and individual workers develop their own strategies for managing the flow of this routine work, but whatever policy is adopted, much social work (including probation officer) time is spent on advising clients about their rights and prospects and negotiating with other agencies: the DSS over benefit delay or suspension; fuel boards which threaten disconnection; and, of course, the housing department. Illustrating the scale of such work, 46 per cent of referrals to the Raploch Estate team in Stirling were found to be primarily about benefits or other financial matters, compared with 29 per cent in the Stirling town team. Raploch team referrals over a six-month period represented one in seven of the estate's population, while the town team's came from only one in 47 of their catchment population.

Whether this activity is best categorised separately as 'welfare rights' or accepted as an integral part of social work, is largely a matter of style and emphasis. Jordan (1987B), for example, has argued that negotiation, counselling and advocacy are fundamentally different activities and that most social workers function only as neutral negotiators rather than partial advocates, whereas Ford (1988) sees these as stages in a continuum. The value of social work intervention on clients' behalf with other state agencies, and also its potentially negative implications, can be illustrated by looking at two areas: challenging housing department decisions about allocation, and applying to the DSS's Social Fund.

Whether to give priority to 'social' factors has long been an issue for housing workers who are concerned with allocation. The Cullingworth committee (CHAC, 1969, p. 38) decided that: 'the assessment of housing need must take account of two major factors: (1) what are the present housing conditions of the household? . . . (2) how well can this household cope with living in these conditions?' That decision introduced 'social' points into the allocation process, and legitimated advocacy by social workers and health workers on behalf of families and individuals who were judged unable to cope. It was an unpopular approach with many lettings officers, who considered it unobjective and therefore unfair (as explained by Spicker, 1986). This helps to explain why attempting to influence housing officers can be such hard work (described by Gill, 1984). However social work persistence can produce results, as evidenced by research into housing departments' treatment of homeless families where social work or medical reports were found to be the only force which could change allocation and transfer decisions (Thomas & Niner, 1989, p. 20).

The disadvantage of this success story is that SSDs are effectively having to certify housing need, as acknowledged by the Central Policy Review Staff (1978, p. 44). They are perforce supporting a 'special needs' approach to housing provision which advantages the most needy only by separating them out from ordinary, generalist processes, and thereby introduces an undesirable element of stigma (Clapham & Smith, 1990). The specialist housing social workers whom we interviewed tried to ensure that formerly homeless families were not identified as clients, because that could mean they were regarded as potentially problematic by housing department staff for many years to come.

Similar dilemmas were raised for social workers by the introduction of the Social Fund in 1988, replacing entitlement to one-off grants for expensive things like furniture with a complicated system of loans and discretionary grants, in which it was believed social workers would play a key role. It was thought social workers would be expected by the DSS to validate financial need and provide information about clients' circumstances. When Social Fund take-up proved to be unexpectedly low in its first year, social workers were blamed, amongst others, for allegedly not co-operating (Stewart & Stewart, 1992B). Obtaining furniture is an important matter for people who are rehoused on to difficult estates, because they commonly have no possessions at all with which to equip their new home.

It is true that social workers (and probation officers) are often asked to support applications for Social Fund 'community care' grants or make referrals to grant-making charities and furniture stores. The evidence is that applications to the Social Fund made with social work support are twice as likely to be successful as those without, but that is not the end of the story. The money granted is often insufficient to meet the need and unsuccessful grant applicants may be persuaded by the DSS to accept loans which they cannot afford. There are no clear qualifying rules and in a cash-limited scheme one client's gain can be another's loss. On the positive side, clients value help in applying to the Social Fund whether or not they receive any money. But the same issues preoccupy social workers as in relation to housing departments: does their intervention label clients as problem claimants; and is there a 'net-widening' consequence from making a special case, whereby claimants must be 'clientised' in order to get the extra money which they need? (Stewart *et al.*, 1990; Stewart & Stewart, 1991)

Developing local services

Another important area of work for social workers on difficult estates is negotiating access for clients to the services provided by their own department. This can be less straightforward than it seems: Seebohm (1968, paras 485–6) noted long ago that what were then described as 'problem areas . . . are inadequately served by social services and . . . there is little mutual aid and few community resources'. Geographical concentration of services away from the areas of greatest need is an aspect of what has been called 'collective consumption' and a subject of sociological analysis (different theories are discussed by Pinch, 1985).

Despite the Seebohm committee's call for a 'generous allocation of resources' in budgets for the new social services departments to reduce the disadvantage of the worst estates, there appears to have been little improvement over the next 20 years. The DoE's study of families in high-rise flats found that when services such as day care for under-fives were put on estates, they were not generally available to estate children, being primarily used for a wider catchment area. Understandably, this was resented (Littlewood & Tinker, 1981, pp. 42–3; also Andrews, 1979, pp. 103–6, drew a similar conclusion).

Gibbons' (1990) research on child care social work found that children from the most disadvantaged families were the least likely to be using day care, and she recommended that practitioners and their managers should make positive efforts to rectify this as part of a preventive strategy for family support. Just such a strategy was pursued by an area team in Wandsworth, resulting in reduced numbers of children in care, but it was increasingly difficult at a time of cuts in local services (Beresford *et al.*, 1987). Delay in providing a day nursery place because of budget restrictions in Wandsworth SSD was subsequently said to be a contributory factor in the death of Stephanie Fox; the inquiry panel considered that, 'the day nursery was the single most important element in (her) protection plan'.

The political popularity of day care declined during the 1980s, along with that of other substantive services directly provided by local authorities. Instead family centres are promoted as the main form of family support service under the Children Act 1989 (DoH, 1991A, paras 3.18–3.24). Family centres originated in the post-war work of Family Service Units with 'problem families'. Family advice centres were endorsed by the Ingleby Committee in 1960. They grew rapidly in popularity during the 1980s, many being run or funded by the big national children's charities such as Barnardo's and the Children's Society, which formerly ran residential homes, as well as by social services departments.

The as-yet-limited research in this area is agreed in distinguishing between two types of family centre: one providing assessment and therapy for a limited number of parents (mothers) who have been referred by statutory agencies, usually with young children 'at risk'; the other offering a more open service to families living in a disadvantaged area, which is often a difficult estate. The first type has been described as 'working class child guidance' (by Downie & Forshaw, 1987) and is ostensibly concerned with surveillance and behaviour modification. The second type is seen as compensating families for material deprivation, by offering good standard play facilities and practical help, and could be characterised as a neighbourhood resource (this is the style advocated by Holman, 1988). However they share essential similarities. Both claim to teach parental responsibility and reduce dependence on state services, thereby following a familial ideology which privatises the consequences of deprivation. Yet practice in both types of centre often seems to question this ideology by seeking to empower clients and encourage real participation. These contradictions are helpfully discussed by Cannan (1990; also Walker, 1991).

A similar distinction between styles of community work has been drawn by Henderson and Thomas (1987). They differentiate 'horizontal' networking in neighbourhoods, which is seen to be in a tradition of community development from 'vertical', 'smash and grab' tactics directed at getting resources or changing policy, which is how they characterise community action. We shall look briefly at each.

Neighbourhood care schemes have mainly been associated with support for older people living alone, but variations have also been developed for families with young children who are isolated on estates. One type which has been particularly successful, in terms of attracting funding and publicity, is the Home Start scheme of volunteer visiting. Trained volunteers, who are expected to be parents themselves, are matched by a paid organiser with families who have been referred mainly by social services. Researchers found the scheme to be more effective than social workers in helping families with severe difficulties (Gibbons & Thorpe, 1989).

Another distinct type of scheme entails group work with half a dozen families who meet together on agency premises where children's play is supervised while their mothers take part in group activities, as opposed to being visited individually in their own homes. Trained non-professionals are used as group leaders. Group members are encouraged to maintain contact with each other outside the regular sessions and some schemes aim to involve lonely adults as well as parents

(Knight *et al.*, 1979). The family groups run by COPE (with DoH funding) are said to: 'give their members the care and support that can be found in an extended family, and encourage the development of informal networks of friends' (Cowan, 1982, p.7). The Home Start volunteers have been likened to concerned relatives who visit to advise about parenting skills, as a grandmother might do.

In both cases the aim was to stimulate caring neighbourhood networks where there would otherwise be isolation, using local people as volunteers. Both types of scheme reported difficulties in recruiting locally, and mainly attracted volunteers from outside the estate or wider area where their client families lived. They had encountered the phenomenon which Abrams *et al.* (1989) demonstrated in researching neighbourhood care: that most volunteers come from middle-class areas while most clients live in working-class districts, such as council housing estates. This inevitably introduces an element of artificiality into neighbourhood networking schemes, whose ability to make real contact with the most marginalised people on difficult estates must therefore be in some doubt.

Neighbourhood care was promoted during the 1980s with all the force of a moral imperative and so too was self-help, when it was consistent with policy objectives to reduce dependence on welfare state services (an NCB resource pack by De'Ath & Webster is detailed in the Resource List). The so-called 'underclass' who are said to inhabit difficult estates are assumed to be incapable of self-help, as we discussed earlier in the chapter. But the inquiry into riots on Broadwater Farm, for example, learned that the estate had a thriving youth association which was run by and for local people. Indeed it was the death of the mother of one of its leading members, while police searched her house, which sparked the disturbances. A researcher on an East Midlands estate which was built in the inter-war period, found as many voluntary associations as he would have expected to find on a 'normal' estate, and concluded that the residents were not difficult people although they may have been difficult as tenants. However these were mainly traditional working-class associations such as the working men's club, and there was an isolationist attitude to activities which were seen as being run by outsiders, particularly if welfare-orientated (York, 1976).

Suspicion of social workers and other professional outsiders who try to stimulate self-help in deprived communities, is one of the issues discussed by Adams (1990), who distinguishes between facilitated and autonomous self-help. A study of self-help groups in inner London found that, as with neighbourhood care, it could not be assumed that professional preconceptions on how to organise services were applicable to conditions on the estates, and many residents were too busy with their own lives to be interested (Knight & Hayes, 1981). Nevertheless there are numerous examples of successful involvement by social workers and other professionals in client self-help groups. The best results seem to come from motivated individuals who are already known from their work in relevant local agencies, such as the initiatives on Wester Hailes Estate in Edinburgh (described by Boyle, 1982).

Turning to community action, we find both different and similar issues to those which have arisen in community development. Initially the problems may be similar: how to stimulate interest in a project and gain access to the client community. Thereafter, activist community workers are more prone to self-examination and their attempts to take accountability seriously can bring its own set of dilemmas.

There is agreement that community action on difficult estates requires an issue. People who have been marginalised will not spontaneously unite to improve their situation and housing issues generally have been a recurrent theme throughout the history of community work. The condition of the buildings and the environment are an ever-present source of dissatisfaction for residents of difficult estates. Thus the Bryants (1982) recount a long struggle over conditions in the Gorbals and Govanhill in Glasgow, as an extended case study in community work; making housing repairs a focus for team-work by unitary methods in an FSU is described by Holder and Wardle (1981); Lees and Mayo (1984) tell how damp and fuel debt were taken up as issues by a resource centre in south Wales; modernising a run-down inter-war estate was adopted as a campaign by Tynemouth Community Development Project (Foster, 1975). Allocation policy is less commonly an issue for existing tenants, or perhaps just less frequently written about, but Kenner (1986) describes a student project investigating the allocation of families with young children to high-rise flats in Bristol.

Community workers are more or less instrumental in their adoption of housing issues as a means of involving marginalised groups in collective action. There is usually a wider objective of empowering underprivileged communities, strengthening their position within the local social structure, or changing the attitudes and policies of dominant agencies. Because of the workers' need to pursue a longer-term agenda, sustaining interest can become as difficult as engaging it in the first place. Initial impetus may be lost when progress is slow, as two FSU workers in Birmingham describe:

> In working for better housing conditions the group is itself undermined by the problems it is confronting: active members accept transfers to other areas or lose heart, some are 'bought off' by their own repairs being done, and many of the other tenants, who are the group's lifeblood, are disillusioned or, understandably, apathetic. (Coffin & Dobson, 1984)

Sometimes tenants feel that their security is threatened by a community worker's intervention with powerful landlords (for example, Croft & Beresford, 1988; Wolinski, 1984, discusses other hazards in work on a difficult estate).

Some community workers have tried to forestall such setbacks and at the same time achieve real, rather than token, participation, through organisational structures in which the worker is formally accountable to a client population and may even be employed by them (for example, Derricourt, 1987; Savill in Henderson *et al.*, 1980). But such departures are unusual and far from the non-radical norm identified by Barr's 1987 survey of community work in Scotland.

Conclusion

We have discussed, in this chapter, the range of ways in which social workers (including probation officers and community workers) are involved in working with residents of difficult estates. Initiatives in developing local services are particularly important in areas where one of the main characteristics is absence of facilities. However the problems associated with living on difficult estates run deeper. Structural and design defects in the houses themselves and, most importantly, the way in which people are regarded and treated just because they live there – these are underlying issues which social work intervention cannot resolve.

Notes

1. There are various handbooks to assist in advising about debt problems mentioned in the Resource List. Step-by-step strategies for debt management are set out in a practical guide by Andrews and Houghton. The regularly up-dated *Fuel Rights Handbook* by Lorber *et al.* explains rights over disconnection and suggests how to negotiate with suppliers and persuade them to observe the code of practice. Both are more comprehensive in their approach to the problem than is common in welfare rights guides, which are often rather mechanistic in their reliance on technical solutions. Green & Maby's *Heating Advice Handbook* is particularly good at suggesting cheap 'do-it-yourself' methods of insulating cold homes and dealing with damp, thereby reducing future bills (Boardman, 1991, is also helpful but more academic – see Bibliography). The operation and availability of specialist money advice centres and self-help credit unions is usefully described by Hinton & Berthoud (1988) and Berthoud & Hinton (1989) – see Bibliography.
2. The complexities of housing benefit are explained in detail in two regularly updated guides by McGurk & Raynsford and Ward & Zebedee (see the Resource List). These also cover poll tax/community charge benefit, and no doubt its council tax successor. The CPAG *National Welfare Benefits Handbook* gives adequate information about both benefits for ordinary purposes.

6

Ill Health, Old Age and Housing

We turn now to the third type of housing problem from our chapter 1 typology, in which the problem lies with the standard of the housing itself or the conditions under which it is occupied. Often the situation is aggravated by the client's deteriorating health. In this chapter we shall seek to illustrate, by reference to the housing of older people, the problems of living in housing which is of poor quality and trying to improve standards.

This country has a history of publicly financed housing projects justified, in part at least, on the grounds of promoting health and wellbeing. While we are sensitive to an accusation of ageism, it is nevertheless true that old people experience more ill health and disability than other age groups. Old people are a huge demographic group and, in numerical terms, form the majority of social services' clients. Traditionally and typically, social workers were and are involved more with council tenants than owner-occupiers, but as we shall see, when old people are the clients concerned, that is not necessarily so.

Cause of ill health?

Medically accepted links between insanitary living conditions and infectious diseases such as cholera and typhoid were the main justification for state intervention in housing in the mid

122

nineteenth century; but the worst extremes of insanitary housing and associated infectious diseases have largely been eradicated in this country. One consequence is that continuing causal connections between housing conditions and ill health have become more difficult to prove. The main contemporary evidence about links between housing and ill-health comes from a variety of specific local studies, which have been reviewed by several academic researchers.[1] However, the findings are ambivalent and inconclusive in many important respects. The most convincing results come not from the manipulation of epidemiological data but from asking people who are affected what they think about their housing, their health and the relationship between the two. This was the method used by researchers in Gateshead and east London (Byrne *et al.*, 1986, pp. 51–2, explained better in Byrne *et al.*, 1985; Cornwell, 1984, chs 1 & 2).

Such a straightforward yet 'subjective' approach is unlikely to satisfy council lettings officers who are asked to give priority to applicants with 'medical points'. Local housing authorities ostensibly give the highest priority to medical reasons for rehousing (AMA, 1985, p. 5; Spicker, 1987, p. 19). Medical points are mainly used within the public sector for transfer, but they can also be necessary for people on the general waiting list in some areas to accumulate enough points for an offer without waiting for decades. Pleas for medical priority, even though supported by a doctor's letter, often seem to be routinely ignored and it is difficult to challenge a refusal with convincing evidence about the effects of housing conditions on an individual's state of health. Doctors tend not to like providing support letters for patients, which can mean that those they do write are inadequately argued and therefore easily dismissed.[2] Following an extensive review, Smith (1989, pp. 34–47) concludes that although medical priority is taken for granted, the difficulties of actually allocating homes in a fair way between the sick and the healthy are neglected. Both groups of applicants are competitors for access to public housing and transfers within it.

Drawing on the various studies already mentioned, we can summarise the factors in and around the home which are likely to affect its occupants' physical and mental health as being: overcrowding; cold and damp; safety; pollution; noise; conflict with neighbours; risk of injury; access to open space and facilities. Illnesses thought to be most associated with housing conditions include: respiratory complaints in children; depression in women; accidents happening to both young children and old people; and hypothermia, particularly in old people and babies. We can add to this the behaviour of both young and older children and of adults as parents. As a means of making sense of some of these findings, we shall concentrate for the rest of this chapter on the familiar situation of old people living in decaying, privately owned housing.

Old people at home

Whether as specialists or in a generic team, social workers are likely to become involved over the housing and health problems of old people. It is useful to categorise how in four ways:

1. With advice and information concerning options available in the district, which is likely to be an essential component of case management. This is particularly important with regard to the plethora of small-scale, mainly local, initiatives that have emerged to help old people 'stay put' in their own home (Harrison & Means, 1990, ch.5). We discuss these under '*Special schemes*' (see p. 129).
2. Social workers can help with support during periods of physical disruption accompanying renovation, as well as the loss and change associated with having to move home – should it come to that.
3. Social workers are expected to contribute to assessments made by other agencies and departments for relevant benefits and services. This is an important area of work, whether with the housing department for a place in a sheltered housing scheme, or a grant from the council for disabled facilities, or the more contentious area of applic-

ations to the DSS's Social Fund for grants and loans. Many of these concerns are considered in '*Resources, rights and realities*' (see p. 132).

4. At a senior or managerial level, social workers may become involved in actually setting-up local projects so that the old people of their area can benefit from improvement agency services, home insulation schemes, or charitable sheltered housing.

But first, what in general terms are the housing conditions of old people and in what circumstances do social workers generally become involved? Retirement pensioners are more likely than any younger age group to be living in housing which lacks basic amenities, such as inside toilet, and is in a bad state of disrepair; and most old people in this position are owner-occupiers. Half of all households without a basic amenity and a third of those living in statutorily unfit dwellings are headed by a retirement pensioner (DoE, 1988). So it is not surprising that social workers are faced with clients in situations like Mrs Aspinall who is 63 and lives with her husband in a nineteenth-century terraced house which they own outright. These housing conditions were probably not causing Mrs Aspinall's ill health but they were certainly impeding its treatment. Her social worker wrote:

> This lady suffers acute attacks of psoriasis and part of the treatment is daily, specially medicated bathing. No bathroom. Has to attend hospital just for daily bath on occasions. Have contacted LA with a view to improvement grant but this will involve the occupiers carrying out extensive repairs and renovations. They are unable to commit themselves to this as husband is near retiring and it would cause financial hardship. Maybe the answer will be to apply for sheltered housing to LA or housing association. Difficult decision for this elderly couple to make. Will need much help and support.

The standard interpretation of housing problems has concentrated on deficiencies such as damp which are associated with ill health and related to low income, but not necessarily to old age. However there are also 'dwelling use' problems which, as Struyk (1987) argues, are age-related. As people grow older, and their capacity for physical exertion declines, the layout of their home may present difficulties which were not experienced earlier in life. Steep stairs, for example, may present quite a problem to someone with rheumatism, a consequence of ageing, while they were scarcely noticed when the person first moved in. Mr Bone lives in a privately rented flat above a shop. Beside the difficulty in climbing the stairs, the flat is damp, which 'adds to his physical complaints'. His wife divorced him a few years ago and he is not doing well at looking after himself and the flat. The social worker rated his basic skills as 'poor'. Housing welfare referred him to social services because he does not want to move away from the small town where he has always lived: 'Client has been offered ground floor accommodation on a bus route outside the area but he has refused this'.

Growing older can also bring loneliness and isolation following the loss of a life-long companion. Women are likely to outlive their husbands: a third of people over retirement age live alone and four-fifths of them are women, mostly widowed (Hunt, 1978, p. 5). It is only in old age that women are likely to become house owners, when husbands die and leave ownership and responsibility for the property to their widows, who will be living on a reduced income (Barelli, 1986, pp. 43–4).

Housing or care problem?

Mr and Mrs Aspinall may have to leave their home and move into sheltered housing; their need is for a bathroom, not protective warden supervision and shelter from life. In such cases, housing problems are being reinterpreted as care problems in the absence of achievable, more appropriate solutions. That is not to say the tenants of sheltered housing do not value or do not like their new home: surveys report that they do (Clapham & Munro, 1990). But often a social worker will put her client's name on the waiting list for sheltered housing as the only apparent means of obtaining accommodation that is safe and of a decent standard.

Nowadays, in most authorities, a majority of admissions to Part III are made in a crisis, often in response to housing emergencies. This could account for research findings that high proportions of old people in residential homes do not 'need' to be there (Audit Commission, 1985; Booth, 1985). Formerly when old people were referred for 'Part III assessment' social workers may have started off with the attitude that admission was more or less unavoidable, and not seriously pursued alternatives. However, in the changing climate of the nineties that is no longer likely to be the case. Social services departments are reducing residential care of the elderly and pursuing various alternatives. Without the option of residential care except for the oldest, frailest and most confused people, it is becoming more important for social workers to seek housing solutions to their clients' problems.

On the other hand the social worker may also be seeking a housing solution where clients' care needs are regarded as dominant. Mrs Ellwood's position is urgent: she has been admitted to a psychiatric hospital at the age of 61 and may never be discharged:

Client chronically sick with pre-senile dementia, requires 24-hour nursing care. Cohabitee wants to have her home and to cope with looking after her, but the house is not suitable. Alternatives: 1) extensive adaptations, local council unhappy about doing this with tenant who has short expectancy of life. 2) Client stays in hospital. Battle with housing department has resulted in impasse. Housing department will not modify a house for such a short time, which is a good prospect family house for another family. The client is deteriorating fast and will not live long.

The housing department's rather morbid attitude is quite understandable in terms of their constraints and responsibilities. The social worker could pursue a transfer to another tenancy which was already physically suitable for the couple, with either the local authority or a housing association.

Without regular home help and community psychiatric nursing services, clients are expected to move to special housing with resident supervision or they are kept in institutions. This situation is a consequence of what Walker (1985) has called the 'care gap': the discrepancy between requirements for domiciliary and day care services, and the level at which these are actually provided for an increasing elderly population. Having to fall back on sheltered provision or residential care in response to what is primarily a housing problem, and expecting clients to move house in order to have their care needs met, are prime examples of misconceived strategies and misdirected effort.

Housing and care problems are clearly inter-related for many elderly clients but they should be dealt with appropriately and in parallel, instead of being conflated and confused. There have been some encouraging signs at the end of the eighties. The white paper which preceded the NHS and Community Care Act stated that 'housing is a vital component of community care and it is often the key to independent living' (DoH *et al.*, 1989, para. 3.5.1). It will take some time before the implementation of the detailed guidance reveals what this might mean, although not too much can be expected without 'ring fenced' funding.

Instances of confusion can be found in the assessments forms used for applications to old people's homes in almost any social services department. Questions relating to functional dependency will typically include: can the client manage to climb the stairs? Can s/he have a bath without assistance?[3] Inability to do these things is regarded as a measure of an old person's frailty or disability, indicating need for care. But it can equally be seen as evidence that the interior design of the house has become inappropriate to its occupant's requirements and should be changed. By this interpretation, the solution could be installing a stair lift and appropriate bath aids. There is great reluctance to change buildings to suit people, particularly old people. In Mrs Ellwood's case the landlord evidently thought this was not worth doing, just to enable an old woman to die at home.

Special schemes

As old people have become a focus of policy attention in the eighties and nineties, benefit take-up campaigns (Age Concern Scotland, 1986) and rights guides have been directed specifically at pensioners.[4] Policy analysts have paid particular attention to elderly owner-occupiers who are richer than old people in other tenures and have the potential resource of the equity value of the house in which they live (Anchor Housing Trust, 1990). This potential for self-help accords with Conservative ideology and policy priorities.[5] Help for the people whose circumstances have been discussed above may come via the various special schemes for improvement and repair which exploit that potential and are currently being extended.

Following DoE-financed research the government have announced long-term funding of local home improvement agencies 'helping elderly people . . . to make use of the assistance available to repair and renovate their homes' (DoE, 1991A, para. 7.68). The most common type of agency services are those which deal with repair, improvement, adaptation; offering help with technical plans and arranging financing for the work, as well as finding and supervising the builder. They are run by local authorities, Neighbourhood Revitalisation Services (NRS) and voluntary organisations such as Care and Repair and Staying Put.

Housing agency services were much promoted in the mid-eighties (HRH The Duke of Edinburgh, 1985, pp. 36–7; IEHO, 1986, p. 11; DoE, 1985B, paras 21–4). The upshot was a government initiative in 1986 to develop 74 schemes with 50 per cent DoE financing and an agreement to participate in a monitoring exercise. The stage was then set for the development of two streams of improvement agencies: first the Staying Put and Care and Repair schemes targeted mainly at old people, avoiding local authority institutions, but exploiting a wide range of financing (Harrison & Means, 1990). Second, the NRS projects which worked on an area basis, used ear-marked improvement grant finance from local authorities and were targeted at low income households in general (Kintrea, 1987).

The monitoring has found the range of performance to be

extremely wide. Agencies relying on loans and old people's savings had difficulty in raising large sums to do major repairs, but were content to do many small jobs. The NRS agencies with access to local authority home improvement grants did the major repair works, but also used owners' contributions averaging 28 per cent of costs for each client. Care and Repair and Staying Put projects relied on two-thirds private funding.

Improvement of the house's physical condition is a different objective from the other major performance criteria: the client's health and independence. The NRS projects were better placed to achieve the former, whilst Care and Repair and Staying Put gave emphasis to the latter. Half of all clients reported increased 'peace of mind' following the improvement work; and they also mentioned improving health and safety.[6] The serious drawback to these otherwise encouraging developments is their patchy cover.

Other special schemes can apply to whole areas of housing.

The large scale slum clearance of the 1960s gave way to renovating housing in General Improvement Areas (although new evidence charts its re-emergence and contests the benign intentions of either policy: see Heywood & Naz, 1990). More recently the government has favoured 'enveloping', whereby the external fabric of a block or terrace is renovated as part of a single contract. By the end of the 1980s enveloping accounted for half of all expenditure in the Area Renewal Programme.[7] It can be efficient and effective, although there are reports of specialist teams of social workers spending their time supporting old people through the building mayhem which, literally, surrounds them (Heywood, 1983).

The government's Home Insulation Scheme (now called Home Energy Efficiency) is a kind of small-scale improvement intended to benefit old people living in cold houses. Loft insulation is promoted in a manner which links housing unfitness with ill health: 'Identifiable benefits [from loft insulation] of increased warmth are reduced dampness, better preservation of the built fabric, fewer health problems and a general improvement of the quality of life' (Treasury, 1989, para. 41; see Resource List, Right to Warmth, for practical guides).

Other schemes offering superficial insulation, draught proofing and poor person's double glazing with cling film, will not remedy serious disrepair but can make life better for the resident of a cold house and reduce heating costs. About 400 neighbourhood energy schemes providing the labour for this kind of service are co-ordinated by Neighbourhood Energy Action (NEA). They are usually based in a community centre using unemployed workers on Employment Training schemes, and give priority to old people living alone. The government's Social Security Advisory Committee has described, in somewhat over-blown terms, home insulation for poor pensioners as a 'primary weapon in the battle against hypothermia' (SSAC, 1986, para. 25). In 1991 the government introduced a new Home Energy Efficiency grant for all low income households. The revised scheme provides labour costs for 'Community Insulation Businesses', although ET schemes are still included. In either scheme, recipients pay 10 per cent or more towards the cost of materials.

These special schemes represent a highly selective approach to social policy whereby relatively few people in selected groups are 'targeted' to receive low budget services, leaving most of the relevant population to go without. Such selectivity, applied to old people in bad housing, has been criticised as both an unsound stratagem and an ineffective method of delivering services, because it neglects or excludes so many people. The particular initiative for severe weather payments which prompted SSAC's comment (quoted above), was condemned by representatives of the Electricity Consumers' Council, the Association of Metropolitan Authorities and the Family Policy Studies Centre as largely irrelevant to solving the problem of cold housing and symptomatic of the lack of a social energy policy. As most British homes are poorly insulated, this is not a minority issue (DoE, 1982, Appendix A; OPCS, 1986, table 5.26).

Housing agency services such as Staying Put and Care and Repair which are 'targeted' on elderly owner-occupiers have been described as another example of the 'special needs' mentality which favours sheltered rather than ordinary housing for old people (Oldman in Malpass, 1986, ch. 7). Special schemes to repair old people's houses are merely substituting for an adequate system of improvement grants and a coherent policy for dealing with housing in disrepair; or compensating for lack of access to decent, safe housing which does not also entail loss of independence. This may be true, but social workers will want to investigate whatever sources of help they can get for clients. So what options should be available?

Resources, rights and realities

A significant proportion of elderly owner-occupiers whose houses are in disrepair cannot afford to maintain them, as they lack either sufficient income or capital, apart from the equity value of their home itself (Oldman, 1990, p. 16). For agency services and other special schemes to be effective they must therefore have resources on which to draw and in practice this means facilitating access to standard sources of finance for owner-occupiers and private tenants living in substandard housing.

In the many parts of the country which are neither endowed with special schemes nor covered by housing advice centres, the social services department may be the only source of advice available to clients. It is therefore important for social workers to familiarise themselves with the type of help on offer and how to obtain it. These resources are provided within national guidelines but with scope for local discretion. Each social services department could usefully provide an information pack for practitioner grade staff on how other local agencies exercise their discretion and to whom referrals should be made. This fairly straightforward task would require periodic updating of information and could be done at team level if higher management were uncooperative – though you might point out how centralised information-gathering would avoid wasteful duplication of effort. The task is more complex, and thus all the more necessary, in shire county departments where half a dozen or more local housing authorities may be involved. There, information might most appropriately be gathered at divisional level.

Local Authority Grants – general

The old system of improvement grants was replaced in 1990 with a new scheme of renovation grants applying to England and Wales (Scotland and Northern Ireland keep the old system of intermediate, improvement, repair and insulation grants). The government claims that 'the [new] system is designed to target resources on the houses most in need of works and the householders who most need help'; so there is a means-test (DoE, 1991A, para. 7.66). There are five types of help: the mandatory renovation grant for poor owners and landlords of unfit houses; mandatory disabled facilities grant for all poor occupiers; a discretionary HMO grant for poor landlords of houses in multiple occupation; discretionary common parts grant for poor landlords; and the innovative but discretionary minor works assistance for poor owners and tenants.

As the system is new, information guides are feeling their way and there is little experience on which to base advice.[8] Owner-occupiers of dwellings over ten years old may qualify for a grant if the property fails to meet a new fitness standard and their resources are below the means-tested level. The grant is discretionary if the dwelling is above the fitness standard. There is no limit to the renovation grant payable. The work will be determined by the condition of the property, as assessed by a local government officer. The amount of grant paid is the difference between the amount that the householder is judged to be capable of borrowing and the cost of the work. The eligibility rules follow those for housing benefit, except that the capital disregard is more generous.

In making an assessment, a home improvement premium is added to the applicant's 'applicable amount' (see CPAG *National Welfare Benefits Handbook* in the Resource List for detailed explanation). If a householder's assessed income is below the applicable amount, the full cost of the works will be met by grant. If, on the other hand, income exceeds applicable amount, a percentage of the excess is assumed to finance a loan to cover the contribution by the householder to the renovation work. If that sum would raise a loan greater than the cost of the works, no grant is payable; otherwise the applicant has to make an appropriate contribution. None of the applicant's outgoings (such as a mortgage repayment) are disregarded in making an assessment.

The disabled facilities grant will involve social workers in making assessments on behalf of the housing authority on whether proposed works are necessary and appropriate to meet the needs of a disabled person, who must already be registered as disabled with social services. The idea is to grant aid works which will enable a person with disabilities to manage more independently in their home, for example: getting into and out of the house; easier access to rooms; suitable bathroom and kitchen facilities; adapting electrical controls; improved heating; facilities which will help a disabled person care for another person who is dependent on them. First, social services will be consulted to assess whether the work is 'necessary and appropriate', then the housing department will judge whether it is 'reasonable and practicable' and administer the means-test.

The minor works assistance is also new and specifically targeted at owners and private tenants on income support, especially old people. Assistance is entirely at the discretion of the local authority. The maximum grant is £1000; it can be used for labour, materials and agency services. There are four purposes: thermal insulation; adaptations to the house of a person over 60, making it safe and secure; enabling a person over 60 to stay, or move in, with a carer by installing extra toilets, baths, cooking or heating facilities; patch repair to make a house in a clearance area weather proof (which could apply to homeless families in short-life temporary accommodation).

Local authorities have initially given very little publicity to the scheme, especially its discretionary elements. The acceptable standard of unfitness often appears to be determined by the financial implication for the local authority. Grant officers around the country estimate the mandatory grants as being between £15 000 and £20 000 each: substantially more than under the old scheme. Hence Birmingham, for instance, is reported as having established a 'very low standard so as to be able to cope with demand and financial issues are driving out professional judgement' (Battersby, 1991).

Leather and MacKintosh (1989) believe that old people will be the demographic group among the poor most likely to benefit, as they should be eligible for 100 per cent grants, with no limit on the cost of the works. But they also point out that if the old person is not an outright owner, s/he will be in a position similar to poor first-time buyers of having to take out a loan, because of the small amount of disregarded income. Clearly the scheme is targeted at people on benefit, but eligibility disappears at a relatively low income level.

It will be those elderly and other low income households who are not 'passported' by something like income support, but otherwise eligible, who may prove most resistant to applying for a means-tested grant with so uncertain an outcome. In those circumstances sympathetic and reliable advice will be valuable. The government believe elderly owner-occupiers should 'receive advice and help at the right time . . . to enable them to go on living in their own homes for as long as possible' (DoH *et al.*, 1989, para. 3.5.1). As social workers are not administratively implicated, they should be well-placed to advise clients.

Using the new scheme

Mr and Mrs Aspinall, who live in an unmodernised Victorian terraced house with no bathroom, should qualify for a grant because of her disability. For disabled facilities and minor works discretionary grants, applications which are supported by a social worker will stand a much better chance than those which are not. And it is a short step from that position for a hard-pressed housing department to decide that it will exercise discretion in favour of individuals only if they are supported by a social worker. This means that social workers are effectively being used to help ration renovation grants.

But what if you are unsuccessful and your advocacy skills let you down? A national organisation such as Disability Alliance or RADAR (details in Resource List) might advise on how to argue about the interpretation of DoE circulars. Alternatively you could expect the department's welfare rights service (if there is one) to deal with this stage for you, as they should be more familiar with the semi-legal documents, but the discretionary character of the most relevant renovation grants makes a rights approach problematic. You may prefer to try local pressure through your own management or an active Age Concern or BASW branch, aimed at getting a more general change in policy arising from the specific case. The client's district councillor could be approached to exercise whatever local political influence s/he may have. In this case, contact should be made by the client, a relative or neighbour, rather than yourself. Politicians of any party are likely to be sympathetic to an old or disabled person living in bad housing conditions.

Whatever increased level of grant is achieved, you and the client will still be left with the problem of how to find the balance of the builder's bill which may be substantial (DoE, 1990B, pp. 35–7). Even in the case of grants for loft insulation and draught proofing, the applicant has to meet 10 per cent of the cost from her benefit income. The DoE assumes that people will seek credit, probably an equity loan based on the value of their house, from a bank or building society, and this is what most of the house improvement agency services recommend. 'Interest only' terms can be negotiated, with the capital being recovered on the death of the borrower or sale of the house and income support claimants can have the interest paid as part of their benefit, with none of the initial restrictions which apply to unemployed mortgage holders. This may be the simplest solution, if it is acceptable to the old person and she and her house are acceptable to the building society.[9] But houses like Mr and Mrs Aspinall's, 'two up, two down' and straight on to the street, may not be regarded as sufficiently desirable in their present condition to merit an equity loan which would be sufficient to pay for the extra improvement work that the council requires.

Financial help from social services

In this situation, or when the sum of money required is too small to interest a lender, social services can themselves provide a loan or indeed pay the balance outright.[10] The Chronically Sick and Disabled Person's Act, 1970, covers *inter alia* the provision of equipment and aids which are not fixed or removable, for example a stair lift, and structural adaptations, such as the installation of a downstairs toilet. Application is usually made through an occupational therapist. The more money you want, the higher you are likely to have to go in the department to seek approval. A budget will probably have been set for the whole authority.

Levels of spending and administrative practices vary widely between social services authorities. It is common for the budget to be spent before the end of the year, even within a few months, and many authorities then keep a waiting list although according to the Act there is a duty to make arrangements once the disabled person's need has been identified. There is therefore scope for questioning any extended delay, even though a further provision to enforce rights to services under the Disabled Persons (Services, Consultation and Representation) Act, 1986, has not been implemented. In 1991 legal action was taken successfully in the high court against Hereford and Worcester SSD for failing to provide a carer under the 1970 Act, when a disabled man's need for one had been assessed.

Financial help from the housing department

Housing departments may also undertake or pay for adaptations under S3 of the 1970 Act. Generally they prefer to do work on their own property using that provision. Difficulties arise when a housing authority has decided not to do adaptations to a dwelling which is occupied by a disabled person, as in the case of Mrs Ellwood, who was likely to die in hospital rather than her own home. As Mrs Ellwood's social worker said, she was fighting a losing battle.

Private tenants

Problems of a different kind may arise when the old or disabled person is a private tenant. Protected private tenants who have full security of tenure can apply for renovation grants on the same basis as owner-occupiers.

The private rented sector still contains some of the worst housing conditions in the country, and old people are over-represented in it. The problems associated with the sector are highlighted in London, which contains a quarter of the country's private rented housing and where a third of all private tenants are pensioners (Pawson, 1986, p. 9). A survey in Kensington and Chelsea, where there are particular concentrations of elderly private tenants and property values are high, reported widespread difficulties in getting repairs done despite the activity of numerous local advice centres. Many old people were too frightened of retaliation by their landlord, based on past experience, even to report that repairs were required (Smith, 1986). This is a good illustration of the reasons which lie behind the extremely low take-up of renovation grants by private tenants. Despite the poor conditions in the private rented sector, councils gave over 100 times more improvement grants to owner-occupiers in London than they did to private tenants (House of Commons Debates 1985, vol.87, written answers, cols 228–30).

London tenants' groups have given shocking descriptions of landlords' treatment of elderly tenants while improvement grant work is being done on their houses. The tenants are harassed out of their homes to give the landlord vacant possession for sale. Recourse to legal sanctions seems to have little effect (Paddington Federation of Tenants' and Residents' Associations, 1981; Federation of Lewisham Tenants' and Residents' Associations, 1984). It is not surprising that advisers like Arden (1985 see Resource List) urge caution in pursuing a private tenant's rights to repair and improve when the landlord is known to be hostile.

The Social Fund – grants and loans

If all else has failed, particularly if an old person's health is not bad enough to make her eligible for help under the 1970 Act, you may have to try those last resort sources of money: charities and the DSS's Social Fund. Charities are unlikely to be interested in helping to pay for building work but they might cover a fuel debt or buy a safe heating appliance for an old woman with no heating in her bedroom, for example.[11]

The Social Fund, like charities, is entirely discretionary, but operates according to its own rules (described in CPAG's *National Welfare Benefits Handbook*, see Resource List). Because it replaced a scheme of entitlement to 'single payments' for things such as house repairs, redecoration and draught proofing with cash-limited discretion, the Social Fund must be regarded as a retrograde step in social security policy, as we have argued and illustrated elsewhere (Stewart & Stewart, 1986 and 1991).

A major rationale for 'community care' grants under the Social Fund is to prevent admission to residential care, and the first priority group is 'elderly people – particularly people who have restricted mobility, or have difficulty performing personal tasks', so long as they already receive income support and have minimal savings (DHSS, 1987, paras 7015, 7162). A CCG can also be paid to assist a carer live with or near their aged relative. One could consider the possibility of putting together a case for both a CCG and a disabled facilities grant in such circumstances.

The DSS expected that 28 per cent of the CCG budget and 10 per cent of the loans budget would go to retirement pensioners, but take-up has been low. A National Audit Office report showed that during the Social Fund's first year elderly applicants in fact received only 12 per cent of grants and 3 per cent of loans, although grants increased somewhat thereafter. They found that: 'elderly owner-occupiers living in houses in disrepair saw a [Social Fund] grant for house repairs as having a direct influence on enabling them to remain in their own home', a conclusion similar to the improvement agency services research (NAO, 1990B, paras 2.22–4, 2.48).

You could argue for a grant to meet the balance of improvement costs for an old person on the grounds that she might otherwise have to enter residential care, at greater cost to the state. It is probably advisable to refer to 'repair' and 'maintenance' rather than 'improvement', as DSS tend not to like the idea of claimants improving their conditions at the state's expense. A CCG can pay for minor repairs up to a fixed amount, which could meet some of the 'grant gap' that may arise in a successful renovation application. An SFO may suggest that some other person or agency should pay, such as social services under the 1970 Act. Your recommendation as a social worker will be important for a client to obtain a grant from the Social Fund, because the SFO will want to be assured about the old person's 'vulnerability' and the likelihood of admission into residential care if a grant is not made to improve her living conditions.

Expectations

There is a popular expectation that social workers will protect older people from the cold, from isolation and from themselves. When an old person is found dead at home, there is likely to be an outcry from the local press asking where the social services were. Hypothermia is an emotive issue which forms a regular subject of parliamentary debate during the winter and it is commonly linked with poverty and bad housing conditions (for analysis of the research evidence see Wicks, 1978, ch. 6).

In the context of these findings and expectations, social work involvement has been planned into some renewal programmes where old people are affected. Some city authorities[12] have at various times, set up joint housing and social work teams in housing stress areas undergoing improvement, as recommended by the DoE (1975, para. 39). Social workers have spent much of their time reassuring elderly residents whose domestic peace has been shattered and persuading them to co-operate with the improvement programme (Heywood, 1983). Another social work role, less popular with the authorities, has been supporting old people's choice to be neither improved, nor moved, nor otherwise interfered with. It is an important principle that people should not necessarily be forced to suffer change because it is thought to be in their best interests, and that risk-taking is both acceptable and desirable in social work with old people (Brearley, 1982, pp. 32–6). Neglecting this principle can seriously threaten clients' right to self-determination and may end by depriving them of liberty, as the next two examples illustrate.

Mr Gibson, aged 66, lives alone in a council flat. His social worker says:

> Client refuses to accept that he has an accommodation problem. Needs total care due to severe physical decline because of alcohol abuse. Short term care has been provided both in social services and the private sector homes – all failed dismally, client refusing to stay. Future plan to work with client and hope to persuade him to be realistic about his circumstances and eventually accept residential accommodation.

Mr Hatton is only in his 40s, but has been admitted to a psychiatric hospital suffering from 'pre-senile dementia'; he is also physically disabled.

> Client was living in derelict house with father; he was found a council flat with his father. When father died, he could not manage alone and came into hospital. Client is confused and needs supervision either in hospital or hostel. Attempted to find well supervised hostel or suitably approved lodgings for client.

Neither of these clients was housed in the private sector and their council landlords may have contributed to the pressure on them to move, particularly if they were in rent arrears or neighbours had complained. While social work clients overall are more likely to be council tenants, studies of old people's housing circumstances in the private sector tend to emphasise their independence and low use of social services. But these surveys also found that client council tenants were just as independent and reluctant to move as were non-client owner-occupiers (Tinker, 1984, pp. 57,58–9; Rose, 1982, pp. 31,34). So the same maxims apply about changing the fabric of the building and its amenities in preference to moving the person – whilst accepting a level of risk as the price of independence.

We should not, however, assume that all elderly clients are content where they are and want to 'stay put'; that would be just as ageist as referring everyone over 60 to sheltered housing. Older people may want to move for similar reasons to younger people. For example, a marriage may break down in retirement, or a bereaved partner may seek a change of surroundings. Mrs Irving,

> presently lives in a large council house in an area she doesn't like, wishes to move to a smaller property nearer her family following the death of her husband. Client is having treatment re her bereavement but still will be better placed nearer family and in smaller property. Borough council have been contacted re present situation and have offered possibility of two flats which will be available shortly for client to view.

The council were not so obliging with 67-year-old Mr Jacobs who,

> lived in new flat with sister and nephew. When sister died he wished to move because flat had unhappy associations. Alcoholism also a big problem which would not be solved by rehousing. Housing Dept. says client was asking for a move to particular block of flats in particular area. His own accommodation was good so he was low priority for a move.

He had to stay where he was. Are the circumstances of Mrs Irving and Mr Jacobs so different that one merits re-housing whilst the other does not? Mrs Irving would release a dwelling for letting if transferred, Mr Jacobs would not, as presumably the nephew would remain. It could also be that in the case of Mr Jacobs, the flat is itself in a difficult-to-let block and so the housing department would have no interest in arranging a transfer for him to a more desirable estate. Releasing a dwelling for letting, especially a large family house, is a crucial factor when negotiating with the housing department. It is also clear from the case notes that Mrs Irving's wish to move is supported by her social worker whilst Mr Jacob's is not, although the reason for wanting to move is similar. In neither case is their physical health being linked to the standard of the dwelling. The housing department's ready willingness to arrange a transfer for Mrs Irving but not for

Mr Jacobs suggests either that they do take seriously social work evidence concerning mental wellbeing, or that freeing a tenancy is an over-riding consideration.

Conclusion

In this chapter we have considered how housing conditions inter-relate with deteriorating health in old age. Apart from the last couple of cases, we have concentrated on the circumstances of old people who own their own homes, for two reasons. First, because it is a complex and unfamiliar area in which social workers are increasingly becoming involved, having traditionally served mainly tenants rather than owner-occupiers. Secondly, it has provided the opportunity to investigate the possibilities and problems of helping people who live in the private sector, which you can then apply to other client groups.

For readers who have just dipped into this chapter of the book, we have already touched on the subject of housing conditions and their effects on health in the context of 'difficult' council estates in chapter 5. The subject was also important in relation to B & B and hostels occupied by homeless families and single homeless people, in chapters 4 and 2 respectively. The theme of bad housing and ill health is inter-woven with each of these different aspects of our original typology, though the circumstances and possibilities for solution are different.

Notes

1. Byrne *et al.*,(1986) ch. 2; Murie (1983) ch. 2; Freeman (1984) ch. 2; British Medical Association (1987) S.3.1; Littlewood and Tinker (1981). There is also a wide-ranging review and discussion paper by Smith (1989). For the British Medical Association, Lowry (1991) has written an accessible discussion of the scientific and medical evidence.

2. See Fisk (1986) pp. 53–5; Fisk (1984) on a survey in Glasgow; and Dunlop (1980) presents another community physician's hard attitudes.

3. Both Isaacs *et al.* (1972) and Social Services Inspectorate (1985) specify criteria for use in assessment, as does Audit Commission (1985) ch. 1, but at a more general level.

4. For examples of rights guides specifically aimed at old people see in Resource List Manthorpe (1986); Grimes (1987); Bookbinder (1987); Goslyn (1988). The continued usefulness of these guides will depend on whether they are updated.

5. Taylor (1987) reviews the literature and for a critical perspective see Wheeler (1986); for government policy see DoE (1985B) paras 13–20; and for comment on that policy see AMA (1986A) paras 2.14–5.

6. The government-sponsored monitoring is extensively analysed in a series of reports: Leather & Mackintosh (1990); Mackintosh & Leather (1990A); Leather *et al.* (1990); Mackintosh & Leather (1990B). Of the agency services which are not being financially assisted by the DoE, 15 have been separately surveyed in DoE (1990B).

7. HM Treasury, 1989, para. 39. The DoE's annual report (1991A) makes no mention of the Area Renewal Programme, but does show in fig. 46, p. 66, that Environmental Improvement Schemes under the Urban Programme were set to benefit 78 726 dwellings in 541 projects in 1989–90.

8. The DoE have published an information pamphlet *House Renovation Grants*, which ought to be available in the usual local public offices like CAB. RADAR have brought out one of their informative guides *The New System of Housing Grants*. Anchor Housing Trust in collaboration with the Institution of Environmental Health Officers have published an information pack *Giving Renovation Grants a Human Face*, which is about the Minor Works Grant: see Resource List.

9. Ennals *Rights Guide for Home Owners*, tells you what to do: see Resource List.

10. This power may be exercised under S2 of the Chronically Sick and Disabled Persons (CSDP) Act, 1970, if the old person is also disabled. The *Disability Rights Handbook* by the Disability Alliance gives details: see Appendix.

11. They are listed in two national directories from Charities Aid Foundation, annual; Directory of Social Change. See also Right to Warmth for practical guides, in the Resource List.

12. Birmingham, Coventry, Ealing, Glasgow, Haringey, Leicester, Southampton, South Tyneside, Westminster and Wolverhampton.

7

The Housing Problem and Social Work

A typology of housing problems was outlined in chapter 1 as an aid to understanding the individual circumstances which clients present to social work agencies. It was argued that problem solving strategies must develop from what is perceived to be the location of the problem: housing conditions, which should be amenable to improvement or adaptation; changing relationships between household members, which commonly end in break-up and the need for someone to move; or an individual's need for support or capacity to cope with their living conditions. It is the third which has probably caused the most debate among social workers: what level of independence should clients be expected to attain, after being institutionalised or otherwise disabled? Why and how should families and individuals be helped to manage in damaging environments where they have no choice but to stay, because of social attitudes towards people with problems?

Throughout the book we have noticed a recurrent association between housing problems, of whatever type, and homelessness. Clients often become homeless, with nowhere at all to live, after leaving their parental home or a sexual partner, and when they have been discharged from an institution. Conversely some of the worst conditions are in housing which has been designated for homeless people – various forms of temporary accommodation, and the 'difficult' estates where formerly homeless people are rehoused with no choice. Some commentators have concluded that relationship breakdown, youth leaving home or the closure of long-stay mental hospitals are in themselves the causes of homelessness and should therefore be stopped. But that conclusion is based on a confusion between the different factors which are involved.

Family conflict and changes in mental health policy may both be the occasion for vulnerable individuals seeking somewhere else to live. If there were ready access to an adequate supply of decent, affordable housing those circumstances would mean only having to change accommodation, not being without it altogether. It is primarily the shortage of such housing which leads to people being put through that process which is called homelessness. So as we argued in chapter 1, it is the quantity and quality of housing and access to it which constitute 'the housing problem' in broad terms. Housing policies which treat housing as property to be accessed, either through market mechanisms or by need criteria, regulating an increasingly residualised 'social' sector, thereby limit the ability of poorer people to resolve their own housing difficulties. Thus homelessness may be explained as a consequence of friction between the pattern of individual circumstances and the grander constructs of housing policy and the market. Wealth buys speedy access to the market but housing policies based on rationing cannot adequately respond to the personal crises of poorer people, and homelessness can be the result.

This book has been long in the writing, mainly due to the rapid sequence of major changes in social policy which appeared during the latter part of the 1980s, for example: a wide-reaching review of homelessness legislation which threatened to end in repeal; deregulation of the private rented sector; the fundamental overhaul of improvement grants; and an explicit attempt to abolish the public sector through rent increases and ever more wide-reaching sales measures. Changes affecting clients' housing prospects were contained in social security regulations and legislation as well as strictly housing policies: restrictions to housing benefit; abolition of board and lodging allowances; age-related income support and the disqualification of those under 18; abolition of entitlement to furniture grants and the introduction of the Social Fund.

On the social work side, policy priorities for the 1990s were specified in a stream of green and white papers and new legislation relating to children's services, community care and criminal justice. We have discussed the relevance of housing issues to child protection work in chapters 4 and 5; to 'care in the community' in chapters 2 and 6; and to the new probation task of supervising 'punishment in the community', in chapter 2. Those areas are of particular concern to social workers because they affect their statutory responsibilities.

But whatever the changing emphases may be in social services and probation policy, it has long been the case that the clients of those agencies are predominantly the poorest and worst housed people in society. Housing issues therefore have lasting relevance for social work practice; restrictions on housing opportunity, influencing the immediate living environment, remain probably the single most important constraint on clients' wellbeing. Although it may be difficult for practitioners to achieve significant change in relation to housing, it is an effort well worth making because any improvement in circumstances is valued.

Developing your own understanding of housing issues will enable you to explain the policy contexts of individual accommodation problems, and apply this to relations with clients. People who are homeless or trapped in bad housing may blame themselves for their circumstances and accept an 'inadequate' label. Helping them to locate themselves in a structural context can increase their self-esteem and ability to cope. This in itself is a valuable application of academic learning.

Resource List

Listed below are all the guides and manuals to which we have referred in the book, with some additions and alternatives (but it does not attempt to be a comprehensive list of such guides). While some of the guides may be out of date by the time you read the book, this list indicates the range of literature which you can expect to find and organisations to approach for new material. Updating information about new editions is given where applicable. The addresses of voluntary organisations are given, where available, because the reader will probably need to contact the organisation direct. No address is given for conventional publishers, as such books should be obtainable through bookshops.

Age Concern (1991) *Using Your Home As Capital* (London: Age Concern England, Astral House, 1268 London Rd, London SW16 4ER [081 679 8000]).

Anchor Housing Trust & Institution of Environmental Health Officers (1990) *Giving Renovation Grants a Human Face* (Oxford: Anchor Housing Trust, 269a Banbury Rd, Oxford OX2 7HU [0865 311511]); relevant to the Minor Works Grant.

Andrews, A. & Houghton, P. (1986) *How to Cope with Credit and Deal with Debt* (London: Unwin); although unfortunately out of print, the advice which this book gives is not out of date.

Arden, A. (1986A) *Homeless Persons: the Housing Act 1985 Part III* (London: Legal Action Group, 242 Pentonville Rd, London N1 9UN [071 833 2931]); legalistic guide for skilled advisers.

Arden, A. (1986B) *The Homeless Person's Handbook* (London: Allison & Busby); for non-experts.

Arden, A. (1989A) *Public Tenants' Handbook* (London: Sphere Books).

Arden, A. (1989B) *Private Tenants' Handbook* (London: Sphere Books).

Bookbinder, D. (1987, new edition due late 1991) *Housing Options for Older People* (London: Age Conern England, Astral House, 1268 London Rd, London SW16 4ER [081 679 8000])

Bull, J. & Poole, L. (1989) *Not Rich; Not Poor: housing options for elderly people on middle incomes* (Oxford: Anchor Housing Trust 269a Banbury Rd Oxford OX2 7HU [0865 311511]); public and private options.

Burrows, L. (1989) *The Housing Act 1988: a Shelter Guide* (London: Shelter, 88 Old St, London EC1V 9HU [071 253 0202]).

Campaign for Bedsit Rights (1991) *Bedsit Rights: a handbook for people who live in bedsits, flatlets, shared houses, lodgings, hostels and 'bed & breakfast' hotels* (London: Campaign for Bedsit Rights, 5–15 Cromer St, London WC1H 8LS [081 278 0598]).

Carew-Jones, M. & Watson, H. (1985) *Making the Break: a practical, sympathetic and encouraging guide for women experiencing violence in their lives* (London: Penguin); well-considered advice by women's aid workers.

CHAR Campaign for Single Homeless People (1991; 12th edition, revised annually) *Benefits: CHAR's Guide to Income Support and Housing Benefit for Single People Without a Permanent Home* (London: CHAR, 5–15 Cromer St, London WC1H 8LS [071 833 2071]).

Child Poverty Action Group (1991; 21st edition, revised annually) *National Welfare Benefits Handbook* (London: CPAG, 1–5 Bath St, London EC1V 9PY [071 253 3406)]; on means-tested benefits; comprehensive, detailed and readable.

Child Poverty Action Group (1991; 14th edition, revised annually) *Rights Guide to Non-means-tested Social Security Benefits* (London: CPAG, 1–5 Bath St, London EC1V 9PY 071 253 3406]).

Children's Society (1989; revised edition 1991) *The Next Step* (London: The Children's Society, Edward Rudolf House, Margery St, London WC1X 0JL [071 837 4299]); young people leaving care.

Clark, M. & Dearling, A. (1986; no plans for a revised edition) *Leaving Home: a training manual for workers with Young People* (London: Shelter, 88 Old St, London EC1V 9HU [(071 253 0202]); separate versions for England, Wales & Scotland.

Coventry Young Homeless Project (1986; no plans for a revised edition) *Home from Home* (Coventry: Coventry Young Homeless Project, Unit 15, The Arches Industrial Estate, Spon End, Coventry CV1 3JQ [0203 715113]); although specific to Coventry and some information will now be inaccurate, this is a lively and accessible workbook style guide for those advising and working with young people leaving home in all circumstances.

De'Ath, E. & Webster, G. (1986; no plans for a revised edition) *Families and Self-Help: A Resource Pack* (London, National Children's Bureau, 8 Wakley St, London EC1V 7QE [071 278 9441]).

Dhoog, Y. & Becker, S. (1989) *Working with Unemployment and Poverty: a training manual for social workers* (London: Department of Social Sciences, South Bank Polytechnic Borough Rd, London SE1 0AA); awareness raising exercises and information.

Disability Alliance (1991; 16th edition, revised annually) *Disability Rights Handbook* (London: Disability Alliance, 25 Denmark St, London WC2H 8NJ).

Dowell, J. et al. (1986; revised edition 1989) *The Emergency Procedures Handbook* (London: Legal Action Group, 242 Pentonville Rd, London N1 9UN [071 833 2931]); detailed reference book for skilled advisers on homelessness, harassment, eviction, disrepair, squatting, protection on relationship breakdown, child care, police station emergencies, emergency money.

Eastwood M. & N. (eds) (1990) *A Guide to Grants for Individuals in Need* (London: Directory of Social Change Radius Works, Back Lane, London NW3 1HI [071 435 8171 or 071 431 1817]); grant-making charities.

Ennals, S. *et al.*, (1990; 8th edition, revised periodically), *Rights Guide for Home Owners* (London: SHAC, 189a Old Brompton Rd, London SW5 0AR [071 373 7276]).

Fimister, G. (1986) *Welfare Rights Work in Social Services* (London: Macmillan); ch. 5 on collecting and organising information, by a leading local authority welfare rights adviser.

Forbes, D. (1988; to be revised in 1992) *Action on Racial Harassment: legal remedies and local authorities* (London: Legal Action Group, 242 Pentonville Rd, London N1 9UN [071 833 2931]); thorough and comprehensive for the skilled adviser.

Fraser, R. (1988) *Tipping the Balance: A Guide to Tenants' Choice* (Salford: Tenant Participation Advisory Service, 48 The Crescent, Salford M5 4NY [061 745 7903])

Goslyn, S. (1988; no plans for a revised edition) *Advising Older People: a guide for housing staff* (London: National Federation of Housing Associations, 175 Gray's Inn Rd, London WC1X 8UP [071 278 6571]).

Green, J. & Maby, C. (1987; to be revised 1992) *Heating Advice Handbook* (London Energy and Employment Network [closed down]; to be published by Neighbourhood Energy Action, 2nd Floor, 2–4 Bigg Market, Newcastle-upon-Tyne NE1 1UW [091 261 5677]).

Grimes, R. (1987) *Law and the Elderly* (London: Croom Helm); ch. 3 maintaining an income and ch. 4 accommodation.

Horley, S. (1988) *Love and Pain: a survival handbook for women* (London: Bedford Square Press).

Housing Support Team (out of print; new edition 1992) *Preparing For Change* (Housing Support Team, 5 Trinity St, London [071 407 0092]); training manual for workers helping people who are homeless to move into their own flats; also useful for leaving home, institutions and moving away.

Hughes, D. *et al.* (1986; no plans for a revised edition) *Housing and Relationship Breakdown* (London: National Housing and Town Planning Council, 14–18 Old St, London EC1V 9AB [071 251 2363]); by academic lawyers.

Institute of Housing (1989) *The 1988 Housing Act Explained* (London: Institute of Housing, 9 White Lion St, London N1 9XJ); guide to 'tenant's choice', housing action trusts, housing associations and deregulation in private renting.

Kurowska, S. (1986) *Information Handling in Voluntary Organisations: an NCVO Practical Guide* (London: Bedford Sq. Press).

Lancaster, E. (1985) *Prisoners and the Welfare State* (Birmingham: Pepar Press); the social security information is out of date but the rest is still useful and not available elsewhere.

Leland, J. (1987) *Breaking Up: Separation and Divorce* (London: Macdonald Optima); by a CAB worker.

Levin, J. (1986) *The Divorce Handbook* (London: Allison & Busby); by ex-director of Legal Action Group

Local Government Information Unit (1990) *The Roof Over Your Head* (London: Local Government Information, Unit 1–5, Bath St, London EC1V 9QQ); an information pack on the Local Government and Housing Act 1989 (rents, repairs, maintenance) for public tenants and councillors alike.

Lorber, S. *et al.*, (1988, 6th. edition, revised annually) *Fuel Rights Handbook* (London: SHAC, 189a Old Brompton Rd, London SW5 0AR [071 373 7276]). Now by Hoffland, A. & Nicol, N. available from CPAG not SHAC.

Luba J. (1989) *Disabled Persons' Handbook* (London: Sphere Books); Part 3 Housing.

McGrath, S. (1990) *Tied Accommodation Handbook* (London: Sphere Books).

McGurk, P. & Raynsford, N. (1991; revised annually) *Guide to Housing Benefit* (London: SHAC, 189a Old Brompton Rd, London SW5 0AR ([071 373 7276]).

McNicholas, A. (1986; revised edition 1989) *Going It Alone: your rights and relationship breakdown: a guide for unmarried women*

(London: SHAC, 189a Old Brompton Rd, London SW5 0AR [071 373 7276]).

Manthorpe, J. (1986) *Elderly People: rights and opportunities* (Harlow: Longman); ch. 2 housing and ch. 4 money.

National Association of Citizens' Advice Bureaux Tribunal Unit (1991; revised regularly) *Maximising Income & Disability Benefits* (Wolverhampton: NACAB Specialist Support Unit, 65 Waterloo Rd, Wolverhampton WV1 4QU [0902 310568]); training packs on income support, family credit, housing benefit and the social fund

National Consumer Council (1991) *An Introduction to Credit Unions* (Milton Keynes: Open University); a learning pack of booklet, audio cassette and notes.

National Council for One Parent Families (1990; 2nd edition, updated) *Information Manual: Guide to Rights, Benefits and Services for Lone Parents* (London: National Council for One Parent Families, 255 Kentish Town Rd, London NW5 2LX [071 267 1361]); loose leaf with subscription for updates.

National Federation of Housing Associations (1990) *Primary Concerns: A Housing Worker's Guide to the Health Services for Homeless Single People* (London: NFHA, 175 Gray's Inn Rd, London WC1X 8UP [071 278 6571]).

National Federation of Housing Associations (1991) *A Guide to the Legal Status of Residents in Shared Housing Schemes* (London: NFHA, 175 Gray's Inn Rd, London WC1X 8UP [071 278 6571]); residential agreements; tenancies; licences.

National Federation of Housing Associations (1991) *Whose Home: accountability to tenants and communities* (London: NFHA, 175 Gray's Inn Rd, London WC1X 8UP [071 278 6571]); a practical guide for housing workers on achieving accountability in housing asssociation schemes.

National Youth Agency (1991) *Leaving Home* (Leicester: National Youth Agency, 17–23 Albion St, Leicester LE1 6GD [0533 471200]); training material and resources for those working with young people.

Pearce, L. (1989) *Mobile Homes Handbook* (London: Sphere Books).

RADAR (1990; periodically revised) *The New System of Housing Grants* (London: RADAR, 25 Mortimer St, London W1N 8AB); the means-tested renovation grants scheme explained.

Randall, G. (1989, revised periodically) *Housing Rights Guide* (London: SHAC, 189a Old Brompton Rd, London SW5 0AR [071 373 7276]).

Resource Information Service (1991) *Hostels in London: a statistical overview* (London: Resource Information Service, The Basement, 38 Great Pulteney St, London W1R 3DE [071 494 2408]); policies, practices and procedures in London's hostels.

Resource Information Service (1991; regularly revised) *London Hostels Directory* (London: Resource Information Service, The Basement, 38 Great Pulteney St, London W1R 3DE [071 494 2408]); comprehensive listing

Resource Information Service (1991, 2nd edition) *Opening Moves 2: the housing, employment, Youth Training and benefit options for 16 and 17 year olds living away from home* (London: Resource Information Service, The Basement, 38 Great Pulteney St, London W1R 3DE [071 494 2408]).

Resource Information Service (1988; no plans for revision) *Women's Housing Handbook (England & Wales)* (London: Resource Information Service, The Basement, 38 Great Pulteney St, London W1R 3DE [071 494 2408]); detailed and comprehensive; benefit information inaccurate.

Right to Warmth guides: PO Box 72 (Glasgow G3 8HH [041 221 7781]

   Unhealthy Homes: research finding on relationships between housing conditions and ill-health (n.d.).

   Porteous, C. & Markus, T. (1991) *Condensation Culture: cause and cure*, guide to conditions behind cold, damp, mouldy homes and an appraisal of remedial measures.

   Fuel: paying the price, guide to disconnection, fuel bills, negotiation and advice (n.d.).

   Warm Homes: the law, guide to legal rights of tenants.

Rodgers, C. P. (1989) *A Guide to the Housing Act 1988* (London: Butterworth).

Sar, E. (1985) *Buying a Home* (London: SHAC, 189a Old Brompton Rd, London SW5 0AR [071 373 7276]).

Scottish Women's Aid (1988 2nd Edition) *Protection from Domestic Violence: a guide to the Matrimonial Homes (Family Protection)(Scotland) Act 1981* (Scottish Women's Aid 13–19 North Bank St Edinburgh EH1 2LP [031 225 3321]); updated loose leaf guide; comprehensive practical readable.

Shelter (1987; no plans for a revised edition) *Care and Repair: a guide to setting-up agency services for elderly people* (London: Shelter, 88 Old St, London, EC1V 9HU [071 253 0202]).

Treanor, D. (1990) *Buying Your Home With Other People* (London: Shelter 88 Old St London EC1V 9HU [071 253 0202]); shared ownership: co-ownership, co-operatives, trusts and leasehold.

Ward, M. & Zebedee, J. (1989, revised periodically) *Guide to Housing Benefit and Community Charge Benefit, 1989–90*, London: SHAC, 189a Old Brompton Rd, London SW5 0AR [071 373 7276]).

Watchman, P. Q. & Robson, P. (1986; revised edition 1989) *Homelessness and the Law in Britain* (Glasgow: Planning Exchange, 186 Bath St, Glasgow G2 4HG); by academic lawyers, for skilled advisers.

Witherspoon, S. (1986; revised edition 1989) *A Women's Place: your rights and relationship breakdown, a guide for married women* (London: SHAC, 189a Old Brompton Rd, London SW5 0AR [071 373 7276]).

Wright, M. (1990) *Young People's Rights* (London: Optima); ch. 7 Leaving Home

Bibliography

Abrahams, C. & Mungall, R. (1989) *Housing Vulnerable Young Single Homeless People* (London: National Children's Home).

Abrams, P., Abrams, S., Humphrey, R. & Snaith, R. (1989) *Neighbourhood Care and Social Policy* (London: HMSO).

Adams, R. (1990) *Self-Help, Social Work and Empowerment* (London: Macmillan).

Age Concern Scotland (1986) *Stake a Claim* (Edinburgh: Age Concern).

Anchor Housing Trust (1990) *Supporting Older People in General Housing* (Oxford: Anchor Housing Trust).

Andrews, C. L. (1979) *Tenants and Town Hall* (London: HMSO).

Archard, P. (1979) *Vagrancy, Alcoholism and Social Control* (London: Macmillan).

Association of Community Health Councils for England & Wales (1989) *Homelessness: the Effects on Health* (London: ACHCEW).

Association of Directors of Social Services London Branch (1985) *Social Services Support: A Code of Practice in the Use of Hotel/ Hostel Accommodation for the Placement of Homeless Families* (London: Association of London Authorities).

Association of District Councils (1987) *Homelessness – Meeting the Tide, Initiatives in District Councils* (London: ADC).

Association of District Councils (1989) *A Time to Take Stock* (London: ADC).

Association of London Authorities (1987) *Tenants in Power: A Radical Alternative to the Government's Public Housing Proposals* (London: ALA).

Association of Metropolitan Authorities (1985) *Housing and Race: Policy and Practice in Local Authorities* (London: AMA).

AMA (1986A) *Less Ruin More Renewal* (London: AMA).

AMA (1986B) *Mortgage Arrears: Owner Occupiers at Risk* (London: AMA).

AMA (1990) *Homelessness, Programme for Action* London: AMA.

155

Audit Commission (1985) *Managing Social Services for the Elderly More Effectively* (London: HMSO).

Audit Commission (1986A) *Managing the Crisis in Council Housing* (London: HMSO).

Audit Commission (1986B) *Improving Council House Maintenance* London: HMSO.

Audit Commission (1989A) *Housing the Homeless: the Local Authority Role* (London: HMSO).

Audit Commission (1989B) *Urban Regeneration and Economic Development: The Local Government Dimension* (London: HMSO).

Avon Social Services Dept. (1989) *Management Review of the Case of Sukina Hammond* (Bristol: Avon SSD).

Baine, S. (1975) *Community Action and Local Government* (London: Bell).

Balloch, S. *et al.* (1985) *Caring for Unemployed People: a study of the impact of unemployment on demand for personal social services* (London: Bedford Square Press).

Banks, C. (1978) 'A survey of the south east prison population' in *Home Office Research Bulletin*, no. 5, pp. 12–24.

Barelli, J. (1986) *Women and Housing Policy* (London: Greater London Council).

Barr, A. (1987) 'Inside practice – researching community workers in Scotland' in *Community Development Journal*, vol. 22, no. 1, pp. 11–17.

Bartram, M. (n.d.) *Consulting Tenants: Council Initiatives in the Late 1980s* (London: Community Rights Project).

Battersby, S. (1991) 'Repair grants – an improvement on the past?' in *Housing*, vol. 27, no. 3, pp. 13–17.

Bebbington, A. & Miles, J. (1989) 'The background of children who enter local authority care' in *British Journal of Social Work*, vol. 19 no. 5, pp. 349–68.

Becker, S. & MacPherson, S. (1986) *Poor Clients* (Nottingham: Department of Social Administration and Social Work, University of Nottingham).

Beresford, P., Kemmis, J. & Tunstill, J. (1987) *In Care and in North Battersea* (Guildford: University of Surrey).

Berthoud, R. & Casey, B. (1988) *The Cost of Care in Hostels* (London: Policy Studies Institute).

Berthoud, R. & Hinton, T. (1989) *Credit Unions in the United Kingdom* (London: Policy Studies Institute).

Berthoud, R. & Kempson, E. (1990) *Credit and Debt in Britain* (London: Policy Studies Institute).

Binney, V. *et al.* (1981) *Leaving Violent Men: a study of refuges and housing for battered women* (London: London Women's Aid Federation).

Black, J. (1991) 'When is a HAT not a HAT?' in *Housing and Planning Review*, vol. 46 no. 2, pp. 10–11.

Black, J. *et al.* (1983) *Social Work in Context: a comparative study of three social services teams* (London Tavistock).

Blom Cooper, L. (Chair) (1987) *A Child in Mind: Protection of Children in a Responsible Society* (London: Greenwich Social Services Dept).

Boardman, B. (1991) *Fuel Poverty: From Cold Homes to Affordable Warmth* (London: Belhaven Press).

Bonnerjea, L. (1990) *Leaving Care in London* (London: London Boroughs' Children's Regional Planning Committee).

Bonnerjea, L. & Lawton, J. (1987) *Homelessness in Brent* (London: Policy Studies Institute).

Booth, T. (1985) *Home Truths: old people's homes and the outcome of care*, (Aldershot: Gower).

Borrie, G. (1982) *Advice Agencies: what they do and who uses them* (London: National Consumer Council).

Boyle, S. (1982) *Mental Health and the Community* (Edinburgh: Scottish Association for Mental Health).

Brailey, M. (1987) *Women's Access to Council Housing* (Glasgow: Planning Exchange).

Bramley, G. & Paice, D. (1987) *Housing Needs in Non-metropolitan Areas: report of research carried out for the Association of District Councils* (Bristol: School for Advanced Urban Studies, University of Bristol).

Brandon, D., Wells, K., Francis, C. & Ramsay, E. (1980) *The Survivors: A Study of Homeless Young Newcomers to London and the Responses Made to Them* (London: Routledge).

Brearley, C. P. (1982) *Risk and Social Work* (London: Routledge & Kegan Paul).

Breton, M. (1991) 'Toward a model of social groupwork practice with marginalised populations' in *Groupwork*, vol. 4, no. 1, pp. 31–47.

British Association of Social Workers (1986) *Housing – Its Effect on Child Care Policies and Practice* (Birmingham: BASW).

British Medical Association (1987) *Deprivation and Ill-Health* (London: BMA).

Brown, C. (1985) *Black and White Britain: the third PSI survey* (London: Heinemann).

Bryant, B. & Bryant, R. (1982) *Change and Conflict: A Study of*

Community Work in Glasgow (Aberdeen: Aberdeen University Press).

Brynin, M. (1987) 'Young homeless: pressure groups, politics and the press' in *Youth and Policy* no. 20, pp. 24–34.

Bull, J. & Stone, M. (1990) 'When relationships break down' in *Housing*, vol. 26, no. 3, April, pp. 13–15.

Butler, A. *et al.* (1983) *Sheltered Housing for the Elderly* (London: Allen & Unwin).

Byrne, D. S. *et al.* (1985) 'Housing, class and health: an example of an attempt at doing socialist research' in *Critical Social Policy* no. 13, pp. 49–72.

Byrne, D. S. *et al.* (1986) *Housing and Health: The Relationship Between Housing Conditions and the Health of Council Tenants* (Aldershot: Gower).

Cannan, C. (1990) 'Supporting the family? An assessment of family centres' in N. Manning & C. Ungerson eds. *Social Policy Review 1989–90* (Harlow: Longman).

Central Housing Advisory Committee (CHAC) (1969) *Council Housing: Purposes, Procedures and Priorities* (London: HMSO).

Central Policy Review Staff (1978) *Housing and Social Policies: Some Interactions* (London: HMSO).

Central Statistical Office (1987) *Social Trends*, no. 17 (London: HMSO).

Central Statistical Office (1989) *Social Trends*, no. 19 (London: HMSO).

Chartered Institute of Public Finance and Accountancy (1986) *Housing Rents Statistics April 1986* (London: CIPFA).

Childs, D. *et al.* (1985) *Citizens' Advice: a study of who uses London's Citizens' Advice Bureaux and the service they receive* (London: Greater London Citizens' Advice Bureaux).

Clapham, D. & Munro, M. (1990) 'Ambiguities and contradictions in the provision of sheltered housing for older people' in *Journal of Social Policy*, vol. 19, no. 1, pp. 27–45.

Clapham, D. & Smith, S. J. (1990) 'Housing policy and special needs' in *Policy and Politics*, vol. 18, no. 3, pp. 193–205.

Clark, E. (1989) *Young Single Mothers Today: A Qualitative Study of Housing and Support Needs* (London: National Council for One Parent Families).

Clark, P. & Huckle, L. (1986) 'Four-point plan to help abused women' in *Social Work Today* 1 September, pp. 11–13.

Coffin, G. & Dobson, P. (1984) 'Finding our hidden strengths' in *Social Work Today* 12 November, pp. 17–18.

Coleman, A. (1985) *Utopia on Trial* (London: Hilary Shipman).

Coleman, G., Higgins, J., Smith, R. & Tolan, F. (1990) *Training and*

Development for Resettlement Staff (Bristol: School for Advanced Urban Studies, Bristol University).

Commission for Racial Equality (1984) *Race and Council Housing in Hackney: Report of a Formal Investigation* (London: CRE).

CRE (1985A) *Walsall Metropolitan Borough Council: Practices and Policies of Housing Allocation* (London: CRE).

CRE (1985B) *Race and Mortgage Lending: report of a Formal Investigation* (London: CRE).

CRE (1986) *Race and Housing in Liverpool: A Research Report* (London: CRE).

CRE (1987) *Living in Terror: A Report on Racial Violence and Harassment in Housing* (London: CRE).

CRE (1988) *Homelessness and Discrimination: Report of a Formal Investigation into the London Borough of Tower Hamlets* (London: CRE).

CRE (1990) *Sorry It's Gone: testing for racial discrimination in the private rented housing sector* (London: CRE).

Conservative Party (1987) *The Next Moves Forward: the Conservative Manifesto 1987* (London: Conservative Central Office).

Conway, J. (ed.) (1988) *Prescription for Poor Health: The Crisis for Homeless Families* (London: London Food Commission).

Cook, T. (ed.) (1979) *Vagrancy: Some New Perspectives* (London: Academic Press).

Cooke, K. & Lawton, D. (1985) 'Housing circumstances and standards of families with disabled children' in *Child Care, Health and Development*, vol. 11, pp. 71–79.

Cooper, D. M. (1980) 'Managing social workers' in B. Glastonbury (ed.) *Social Work in Conflict: the Practitioner and the Bureaucrat* (London: Croom Helm).

Corden, J. & Clifton, M. (1985) 'Helping socially isolated prisoners' in *British Journal of Social Work*, vol. 15, pp. 331–50.

Corney, R. H. (1981) 'Client perspectives in a general practice attachment' in *British Journal of Social Work*, vol. 11 no. 2, pp. 159–70.

Cornwell, J. (1984) *Hard-earned Lives: accounts of health and illness from east London* (London: Tavistock).

Council of Mortgage Lenders (1991) 'Mortgage Arrears and possession statistics', Press release, 14 February (London: Council of Mortgage Lenders).

Cowan, J. (1982) *People Cope: Family Groups in Action* (London: COPE).

Cox, A. and Cox, G. (1977) *Borderlines: A Partial View of Detached Work with Homeless Young People* (Manchester: Youth Development Trust).

Croft, S. & Beresford, P. (1988) 'Being on the receiving end: lessons for community development and user involvement' in *Community Development Journal*, vol. 23, no. 4.

Currie, H. and Miller, B. (1987) *A Home of My Own: A Survey and Review of Multiple Occupancy in Scotland* (Edinburgh: Scottish Council for Single Homeless).

Damer, S. (1989) *From Moorepark to 'Wine Alley': The Rise and Fall of a Glasgow Housing Scheme* (Edinburgh: Edinburgh University Press).

Dant, T. & Deacon, A. (1989) *Hostels to Homes? The Rehousing of Homeless Single People* (Aldershot: Avebury).

Department of Education and Science, Review Group on the Youth Service (1983) *Young People in the 80s: A Survey* (London: HMSO).

Department of the Environment, Department of Health & Social Security and Welsh Office (1974) *Homelessness*, circular 18/74 (London: HMSO).

Department of the Environment (1975) *Housing Action Areas, Priority Neighbourhoods and General Improvement Areas*, circular 14/75 (London: HMSO).

Department of the Environment (1982) *English House Condition Survey 1981*, Part 1 (London: HMSO).

Department of the Environment (1985A) *An Inquiry into the Condition of the Local Authority Housing Stock in England: 1985* (London: DoE).

Department of the Environment (1985B) *Home Improvement: a new approach*, Cmnd. 9513 (London: HMSO).

Department of the Environment (1987) *Housing: the Government's Proposals*, Cm. 214 (London: HMSO).

Department of the Environment (1988) *English House Condition Survey 1986* (London: HMSO).

Department of the Environment (1990A) *Hulme Study. Stage 1: Initial Action Plan* (London: HMSO).

Department of the Environment (1990B) *'Unassisted' Agency Services: a study of agency services set up outside the DoE & WO initiative* (London: HMSO).

Department of the Environment (1991A) *Annual Report 1991*, Cm. 1508 (London: HMSO).

Department of the Environment, Department of Health and Welsh Office (1991B) *Homelessness Code of Guidance for Local Authorities: Part III of the Housing Act 1985*, 3rd edition (London: HMSO).

Department of the Environment (1991C) *Community Care – Draft Circular to Housing Authorities* (London: DoE).

Department of the Environment (quarterly), *Housing and Construction Statistics* (London: HMSO).

Department of the Environment (quarterly; prior to 1985 half yearly) *Local Authorities' Action Under the Homelessness Provision of the 1985 Housing Act: England*, formerly titled prior to April 1987 *Homeless Households Reported by Local Authorities in England* (London: DoE).

Department of the Environment (quarterly) *Local Housing Statistics* (London: HMSO).

Department of Health (1988) *Protecting Children: A Guide for Social Workers Undertaking a Comprehensive Assessment* (London: HMSO).

Department of Health *et al.* (1989) *Caring for People: community care in the next decade and beyond*, Cm. 849 (London: HMSO).

Department of Health (1990) *Community Care in the Next Decade and Beyond: Policy Guidance* (London: HMSO).

Department of Health (1991A) *The Children Act 1989 Guidance and Regulations vol. 2 Family Support, Day Care and Educational Provision For Young Children* (London: HMSO).

Department of Health (1991B) *The Children Act 1989 Guidance and Regulations vol. 3 Family Placements* (London: HMSO).

Department of Health (1991C) *Working Together*, revised edition (London: HMSO).

Department of Health & Social Security (1985) *Review of Child Care Law: report to ministers of an interdepartmental working party* (London: HMSO).

Department of Health & Social Security (1986) *Supplementary Benefit Board and Lodging Allowances: Monitoring the Impact of the 1985 Changes* (London: DHSS).

Department of Health & Social Security (1987) *The Social Fund Manual* (London: HMSO).

Derricourt, N. (1987) 'Where the tenant is boss' in *Community Care*, 11 June, pp. 14–17.

Dillon, M. & Parker, J. (1988) 'Faith, hope and charity?' in S.Becker & S.MacPherson (eds) *Public Issues Private Pain* (London: Care Matters Ltd).

Dodd, T. & Hunter, P. (1990) *Trading Down and Moves Out of Owner Occupation* (London: HMSO).

Doling, J. *et al.* (1986) 'Conflicts in organizational objectives: the management of local authorities' mortgage arrears' in *Local Government Studies* March–April pp. 67–76.

Doling, J. & Wainwright, S. (1989) 'Public and private debt' in *Housing Review*, vol. 38, no. 3, May–June, pp. 80–2.

Downie, A. & Forshaw, P. (1987) 'Family centres' in *Practice*, vol. 1 no. 2, pp.140–7.

Drake, M., O'Brien, M. & Biebuyck, T. (1981) *Single and Homeless* (London: HMSO).

Dunleavy, P. (1981) *The Politics of Mass Housing in Britain, 1945–57* (Oxford University Press).

Dunlop, J. M. (1980) 'A doctor looks at housing' in *Housing* vol. 16, no. 3, March, pp. 13–5.

Engels, F. (1872) *The Housing Question* (Moscow: Progress Publishers; there is a 1975 edition).

Evans, A. & Duncan, S. (1988) *Responding to Homelessness: Local Authority Policy and Practice* (London: HMSO).

Fairhead, S. (1981) *Persistent Petty Offenders*, Home Office Research Study no. 66 (London: HMSO).

Federation of Lewisham Tenants' and Residents' Associations (1984) *Health and Housing in Lewisham: a report on Lewisham Council's environmental health policies and practices* (London: Lewisham FTRA).

Fellows, G. (1979) 'Social work in a single homeless team' in Marshall, M., Mitchell, G. & Sackville, A. (eds) *Social Work in Action* (Birmingham: BASW).

Fisk, M. J. (1984) 'Medical assessments and priority for housing' in *Health Bulletin*, vol. 42, no. 2, pp. 92–6.

Fisk, M. J. (1986) *Independence and the Elderly* (London: Croom Helm).

Folkard, M. S. *et al.* (1976) *IMPACT Intensive Matched Probation and After-care Treatment*, vol. 2 (London: HMSO).

Ford, J. (1988) 'Negotiation (counselling and advocacy): a response to Bill Jordan' in *British Journal of Social Work*, vol. 18, pp. 57–62.

Ford, J. (1991) *Consuming Credit: Debt and Poverty in the UK* (London: CPAG).

Forrest, R. & Murie, A. (1988) *Selling the Welfare State* (London: Routledge).

Foster, J. (1975) 'Working with tenants: two case studies' in Lees, R. & Smith, G., *Action-Research in Community Development* (London: Routledge).

Fowler, G. (1987) 'Getting to grips with welfare' in *Probation Journal*, vol. 34, no. 4, pp. 142–4.

Francis, L. J. (1982A) *Youth In Transit: a profile of 16–25 year olds* (Aldershot: Gower).

Francis, L. J. (1982B) *Experience of Adulthood: a profile of 26–39 year olds* (Aldershot: Gower).

Freeman, H. (ed.) (1984) *Mental Health and the Environment* (London: Churchill Livingstone).

Furlong, A. & Cooney, G. (1990) 'Getting on their bikes: teenagers leaving home in Scotland in the 1980s' in *Journal of Social Policy*, vol. 19, no. 4, pp. 535–52.

Garside, P. L., Grimshaw, R. W. & Ward, F. J. (1990) *No Place Like Home: The Hostels Experience* (London: HMSO).

Gibbons, J. (1990) *Family Support and Prevention: Studies in Local Areas* (London: HMSO).

Gibbons, J. & Thorpe, S. (1989) 'Can voluntary support projects help vulnerable families? The work of Home Start' in *British Journal of Social Work*, vol. 19, no. 3, pp. 189–202.

Gifford, L. (Chair) (1986) *The Broadwater Farm Inquiry* (London: Karia Press).

Gill, O. (1984) 'Pressure points' in *Community Care*, 22 November, pp. 22–23.

Glampson, A. & Goldberg, E. M. (1976) 'Post Seebohm social services: the consumer's viewpoint' in *Social Work Today*, vol. 8, no. 6, 9 November, pp. 7–12.

Glendinning, C. (1990) 'Dependency and interdependency: the incomes of informal carers and the impact of social security' in *Journal of Social Policy*, vol. 19, no. 4, October, pp. 445–467.

Goldberg, E. M. & Warburton, R. W. (1979) *Ends and Means in Social Work: the development of a case review system for social workers* (London: Allen & Unwin).

Greater London Council, Controller of Housing and Technical Services (1985) *Relationship Breakdown: the implications for local authority tenancies and the impact of the 1980 Housing Act*, Housing Committee/Women's Committee report 17, September (London: GLC).

Griffin, C. (1985) *Typical Girls?* (London: Routledge and Kegan Paul).

Hadley, R. & McGrath, M. (1984) *When Social Services are Local: the Normanton experience* (London: Allen & Unwin).

Hales, J. & Shaw, S. (1990) *New Lettings by Housing Associations* (London: HMSO).

Haley, J. (1980) *Leaving Home: The Therapy of Disturbed Young People* (New York: McGraw Hill).

Hanmer, J. & Statham, D. (1988) *Women and Social Work: Towards a Woman-Centred Practice* (London: Macmillan).

Harloe, M. & Horrocks, M. (1974) 'Responsibility without power: the case of social development' in D. Jones & M. Mayo (eds) *Community Work One* (London: Routledge).

Harrison, L & Means, R. (1990) *Housing: the essential element in community care; the role of 'Care and Repair' and 'Staying Put Projects'* (Oxford: Anchor Housing Trust).

Health Visitors' Association & BMA General Medical Services Committee (1988) *Homeless Families and Their Health* (London: British Medical Association).

Hearn, B. & Thomson, B. (1987) *Developing Community Social Work in Teams: A Manual for Practice* (London: National Institute for Social Work).

Hearnden, D. (1984) *Co-ordinating Housing and Social Services: From Good Intentions to Good Practice* (London: Centre for Policy on Ageing).

Henderson, J. & Karn, V. (1987) *Race, Class and State Housing: inequality and the allocation of public housing in Britain* (Aldershot: Gower).

Henderson, M. & Argyle, M. (1985) 'Source and nature of social support given to women at divorce/separation' in *British Journal of Social Work*, vol. 15, pp. 57–65.

Henderson, P. (1986) *Community Work and the Probation Service* (London: National Institute for Social Work).

Henderson, P., Jones, D. & Thomas, D. N. (1980) *The Boundaries of Change in Community Work* (London: Allen & Unwin).

Henderson, P. & Thomas, D. N. (1987) *Skills in Neighbourhood Work* (London: Allen & Unwin).

Her Majesty's Inspectorate (1990) *A Survey of the Education of Children Living in Temporary Accommodation, April–December 1989* (London: Department of Education).

Heywood, F. (1983) 'Envelope game' in *Social Work Today*, 26 July, p. 6.

Heywood, F. & Naz, M. R. (1990) *Clearance: the view from the street* (Birmingham: Community Forum, Shape Centre).

Hill, M. & Laing, P. (1979) *Social Work and Money* (London: Allen & Unwin).

Hine, J. *et al.* (1976) *Accommodation Problems and Probation Practice* (Sheffield: South Yorkshire Probation and After-care Service).

Hinton, T. & Berthoud, R. (1988) *Money Advice Services* (London: Policy Studies Institute).

Holder, D. & Wardle, M. (1981) *Teamwork and the Development of a Unitary Approach* (London: Routledge).

Holman, B. (1988A) *Putting Families First: Prevention and Child Care* (London: Macmillan).

Holman, B. (1988B) 'Research from the underside' in *Community Care*, 18 February, pp. 24–26.

Home Office & Scottish Office (1985) *Review of Public Order Law*, Cmnd.9510 (London: HMSO).

Home Office (1988) *Punishment, Custody and the Community*, Cm.424 (London: HMSO).

Home Office (1990) *Supervision and Punishment in the Community*, Cm.966 (London: HMSO).

Hooper, D., Coleman, J. & Ineichen, B. (1978) 'Social work intervention on a new housing estate' in *British Journal of Social Work*, vol. 8, no. 4.

Hope, T. & Shaw, M. (eds) (1988) *Communities and Crime Reduction* (London: HMSO).

House of Commons Home Affairs Committee (1986) *Racial Attacks and Harassment*, 3rd report, session 1985–86, HCP 409 (London: HMSO).

House of Commons Scottish Affairs Committee (1984) *Dampness in Housing*, 1st report, session 1983–4, HCP 206–I (London: HMSO).

House of Commons Social Security Committee (1991) *Changes in Maintenance Arrangements: the white paper 'Children Come First' and the Child Support Bill*, session 1990–1, HCP 277–II (London: HMSO).

House of Commons Social Services Committee (1984) *Children In Care*, 2nd report, session 1983–4, HCP 360–I (London: HMSO).

HRH The Duke of Edinburgh (Chair) (1985) *Inquiry Into British Housing* (London: National Federation of Housing Associations).

Hudson, B. (1986) 'In pursuit of co-ordination: housing and the personal social services' in *Local Government Studies*, March/April, pp. 53–66.

Hunt, A. (1978) *The Elderly at Home* (London: HMSO).

Hutchinson-Reis, M. (1986) 'After the uprisings – social work on Broadwater Farm' in *Critical Social Policy*, vol. 6, no. 2, pp. 70–79.

Inner London Education Authority (1987A) *Homeless Families – Report to the Director of Education, Schools* (London: ILEA).

Inner London Education Authority (1987B) *Homeless Families: Implications for the Education Welfare Service* (London: ILEA).

Institute of Environmental Health Officers (1986) *Renovation Grant and Associated Policies in Local Authorities* (London: IEHO).

Institute of Housing (1987) *Preparing for Change: Future Use, Control and Management* (London: Institute of Housing).

Isaacs, B. *et al.* (1972) *The Measurement of Need in Old People* (Edinburgh: Scottish Home and Health Department).

Islington Social Services Dept. (1989) *Liam Johnson Review: Report of Panel of Inquiry* (London Borough of Islington).

Jacobs, S. (1976) *The Right to a Decent House* (London: Routledge and Kegan Paul).

Jay, P. (1979) *Report of the Committee of Enquiry into Mental Handicap Nursing and Care*, Cmnd. 7468–1 (London: HMSO).

Jeffrey, R. (1979) 'Normal rubbish: deviant patients in casualty departments' in *Sociology of Health and Illness*, vol. 1, no. 1, pp. 90–107.

Jones, G. (1987) 'Leaving the parental home: an analysis of early housing careers' in *Journal of Social Policy*, vol. 16, no. 1, pp. 49–74.

Jordan, B. (1979) *Helping in Social Work* (London: Routledge).

Jordan, B. (1987A) *Rethinking Welfare* (Oxford: Blackwell).

Jordan, B. (1987B) 'Counselling, advocacy and negotiation' in *British Journal of Social Work*, vol. 17, pp. 135–46.

Karn, V. *et al.* (1985) *Home Ownership in the Inner City* (Aldershot: Gower).

Kay, A. & Legg, C. (1986) *Discharged to the Community: A Review of Housing and Support in London for People Leaving Psychiatric Care* (London: Housing Research Group, City University).

Kenner, C. (1986) *Whose Needs Count? Community Action for Health* (London: Bedford Square Press).

Kent County Council, Officer Working Group (1981) *The Operation of the Housing (Homeless Persons), Act 1977 in Kent* (Maidstone: Kent Social Services Department).

Kintrea, K. (1987) *Arresting Decay in Owner Occupied Housing? The Neighbourhood Revitalisation Services scheme: a preliminary analysis* (Glasgow: Centre for Housing Research, University of Glasgow).

Knight, B., Gibson, M. & Grant, S. (1979) *Family Groups in the Community* (London: London Voluntary Service Council).

Knight, B. & Hayes, R. (1981) *Self-Help in the Inner City* (London: London Voluntary Service Council).

Kraemer, S. (1982) 'Leaving home, and the adolescent family therapist' in *Journal of Adolescence*, vol. 5 no. 1, pp. 51–63.

Labour Housing Group (1984) *Right to a Home* (Nottingham: Spokesman Books).

Law Centres Federation (1986) *Civil Justice and Housing Disputes: a law fit to live in?* (London: Law Centres' Federation).

Law Commission (1987) *Landlord and Tenant: reform of the law*, Cm. 145 (London: HMSO).

Leather, P. & Mackintosh, S. (1989) 'Means-testing improvement grants' in *Housing Review*, vol. 38, no. 3, May–June, pp. 77–9.

Leather, P. & Mackintosh, S. (1990) *Monitoring Assisted Agency*

Services: Part I – Home Improvement Agencies – an evaluation of performance (London: HMSO).

Leather, P. *et al.* (1990) *Monitoring Assisted Agency Services: Part III – the detailed case studies* (London: HMSO).

Lees, R. & Mayo, M. (1984) *Community Action for Change* (London: Routledge & Kegan Paul).

Lewis, P. (1986) 'Less work, less money, less hope' in *Poverty*, no. 62, pp. 15–9.

Liddiard, M. & Hutson, S. (1991) 'Homeless young people and runaways – agency definitions and processes' in *Journal of Social Policy*, vol. 20, no. 3, pp. 365–88.

Limehouse Fields Tenants Association (1987) *Tenants Tackle Racism* (London: Dame Colet House).

Littlewood, J. & Tinker, A. (1981) *Families in Flats* (London: HMSO).

Logan, P. (1989) *A Life to be Lived: Homelessness and Pastoral Care* (London: Darton Longman & Todd).

London Boroughs Association (1989) *Giving Hope to London's Homeless – The Way Forward* (London: LBA).

London Research Centre (1988) *Access to Housing: a report based on the results of the London Housing Survey 1986–7* (London: London Research Centre).

Lovell, B. (1986) 'Health visiting homeless families' in *Health Visitor*, vol. 59, pp. 334–6.

Lowry, S. (1991) *Housing and Health* (London: British Medical Journal).

McCafferty, P. & Riley, D. (1989) *A Study of Co-operative Housing* (London: HMSO).

McGibbon, A. *et al.* (1989) *What Support? an exploratory study of council policy and practice, and local support services in the area of domestic violence within Hammersmith and Fulham* (London: Community Research Advisory Centre, Polytechnic of North London).

Mackintosh, S. & Leather, P. (1990A) *Monitoring Assisted Agency Services: Part II – people, properties and performance* (London: HMSO).

Mackintosh, S. & Leather, P. (1990B) *Monitoring Assisted Agency Services: Part IV – monitoring performance* (London: HMSO).

Maclean, M. (1991) *Surviving Divorce: women's resources after separation* (London: Macmillan).

Maclennan, D., Gibb, K. & More, A. (1990) *Paying for Britain's Housing* (York: Joseph Rowntree Foundation).

Macnicol, J. (1987) 'In pursuit of the underclass' in *Journal of Social Policy*, vol. 16, no. 3, pp. 293–318.

Malpass, P. (ed.) (1986) *The Housing Crisis* (London: Croom Helm).

Malpass, P. (1990) *Reshaping Housing Policy: subsidies, rents and residualisation* (London: Routledge).

Martin, C. J. (1989) 'Researching the obvious and influencing the influentials' in *Local Government Policy Making*, vol. 16, pp. 47–52.

Masterson, A. (1982) *A Place of My Own: Young People Leaving Home – A Youth Work Approach* (Manchester: Greater Manchester Youth Association).

Mattinson, J & Sinclair, I. (1979) *Mate and Stalemate; working with marital problems in a social services department* (Oxford: Blackwell).

May, J. S. & Whitbread, A.W. (1975) 'The downward spiral: a study of homeless families in Warwickshire' in *Bulletin of the Clearing House for Local Authority Social Services Research*, no. 5, pp. 3–64.

Merrett, S. (1985) *The Right to Rent: a feasibility study* (London: Greater London Council).

Merrison Report (1979) *Report of the Royal Commission on the National Health Service*, Cmnd.7615 (London: HMSO).

Minford, P. *et al.* (1987) *The Housing Morass: regulation, immobility and unemployment* (London: Institute of Economic Affairs).

Minns, R. (1972) 'Homeless families and some organisational determinants of deviancy' in *Policy and Politics*, vol. 1, no. 1, pp. 1–21.

Moore, J., Canter, D., Stockley, D. & Drake, M. (1991) *Faces of Homelessness* (Guildford: Psychology Department, University of Surrey).

Morfett, R. & Pidgeon, J. (1991) 'Unity in action' in *Social Work Today*, 10 January, pp.16–17.

MORI (1990) *Income Support: A Survey of Low Income Families* (London: National Audit Office).

Morris Committee, Scottish Development Department (1975) *Housing and Social Work, A Joint Approach* (Edinburgh: HMSO).

Murie, A. (1983) *Housing Inequality and Deprivation* (London: Heinemann).

Murray, C. (1990) *The Emerging British Underclass* (London: Institute of Economic Affairs).

National Association of Citizens' Advice Bureaux (1986) *Annual Report 1985–86* (London: NACAB).

National Association of Probation Officers, Social Policy Committee (1985) *Housing Practice in the Probation Service* (London: NAPO).

National Audit Office (1989) *Department of the Environment: housing needs and allocations*, HCP 567 (London: HMSO).

National Audit Office (1990A) *Homelessness*, session 1989–90, HCP 622 (London: HMSO).

National Audit Office (1990B) *The Elderly: information requirements for supporting the elderly and implications of personal pensions for the National Insurance Fund*, session 1990–91, HCP 55 (London: HMSO).

Niner, P. (1989) *Homelessness in Nine Local Authorities: Case Studies of Policy and Practice* (London: HMSO).

Nottingham Probation Housing Team (1989) 'Poverty and accommodation: is "resettlement" feasible any longer?' in *Probation Journal*, vol. 36, no. 4, pp. 171–6.

Noyes, P. (1991) *Child Abuse: A Study of Inquiry Reports 1980–1989* (London: HMSO).

Office of Population Censuses and Surveys (1986) *General Household Survey 1984* (London: HMSO).

Oldman, C. (1990) *Moving in Old Age: new directions in housing policies* (London: HMSO).

Oliver, J.P.J. *et al.* (1989) *Mental Health Casework* (Manchester University Press).

O'Malley, J. (1977) *The Politics of Community Action* (Nottingham: Spokesman Books).

One Plus & Shelter (1988) *Out in the Cold: single parents and housing policies* (Glasgow: One Plus & Shelter).

Owens, J. (1988) 'Housing and social work, pulling together' in *Housing*, vol. 24, no. 2, pp. 20–1.

Packman, J., Randall, J. & Jacques, N. (1986) *Who Needs Care? Social Work Decisions About Children* (Oxford: Blackwell).

Paddington Federation of Tenants' and Residents' Associations (1981) *Taken for Granted: improvement grants in Westminster* (London: PFTRA).

Pahl, J. (1978) *A Refuge for Battered Women: a study of the rôle of a women's centre* (London: HMSO).

Pahl, J. (ed.) (1985) *Private Violence and Public Policy: the needs of battered women and response of the public services* (London: Routledge and Kegan Paul).

Parsons, R.J.S. (1983) 'Social work with single parent families: consumer views' in *British Journal of Social Work*, vol. 13, no. 5, October, pp. 539–59.

Pawson, H. (1986) *Private Tenants in London: the GLC survey 1983–4* (London: Greater London Council).

Pawson, H. and Tuckley, W. (1986) *The Housing Needs Survey: a*

Comprehensive Method of Assessing Housing Requirements (London: London Research Centre).

Perring, C., Twigg, J. & Atkin, K. (1990) *Families Caring for People Diagnosed as Mentally Ill: The Literature Re-examined* (London: HMSO).

Phillips, D. (1986) *What Price Equality? A Report on the Allocation of GLC Housing in Tower Hamlets* (London: Greater London Council).

Phoenix, A. (1991) *Young Mothers?* (Cambridge: Polity Press).

Pilkington, E. & Kendrick, T. (1987) 'Area repairs: a new deal for tenants or papering over the cracks?' in P. Hoggett & R. Hambleton (eds) *Decentralisation and Democracy: Localising Public Services* (Bristol: School for Advanced Urban Studies, Bristol University).

Pinch, S. (1985) *Cities and Services: The Geography of Collective Consumption* (London: Routledge).

Pinto, R. R. (1991) 'Central/local interaction in renovating run-down estates – the view of housing authorities on the Estate Action Initiative' in *Local Government Studies*, January–February, pp. 45–62.

Platt, S. D., Martin, C. J., Hunt, S. M. & Lewis, C. (1989) 'Damp housing, mould growth and symptomatic health state' in *British Medical Journal*, no. 298, pp. 1673–8.

Police Monitoring and Research Group (1986) *Police Response to Domestic Violence* (London: London Strategic Policy Unit).

Power, A. (1987) *Property Before People: the management of twentieth century council housing* (London: Allen & Unwin).

Power, A. (1991) *Housing Management: A Guide to Quality and Creativity* (Harlow: Longman).

Prescott-Clarke, P. *et al.* (1988) *Queuing for Housing: a study of council housing waiting lists* (London: HMSO).

Purkiss, E. & Sim, D. (1985) *Mortgage Default in Glasgow*, Housing Department Research memo. no. 5 (Glasgow: Glasgow District Council).

Ramsay, E. & Smith, R. (1987) *Housing Associations in Wales* (London: National Federation of Housing Associations).

Randall, G., Francis, D. & Brougham, C. (1982) *A Place For the Family: Homeless Families in London* (London: SHAC).

Rao, N. (1990) *The Changing Role of Local Housing Authorities* (London: Policy Studies Institute).

Rauta, I. (1986) *Who Would Prefer Separate Accommodation?* (London: HMSO).

Reynolds, F. (1986) *The Problem Estate* (Aldershot: Gower).

Richardson, A. & Ritchie, J. (1989) *Letting Go: Dilemmas for Parents Whose Son or Daughter has a Mental Handicap* (Milton Keynes: Open University Press).

Ricketts, M. (1986) *Lets Into Leases: the political economy of rent deregulation* (London: Centre for Policy Studies).

Riley, D. & Shaw, M. (1985) *Parental Supervision and Juvenile Delinquency*, Home Office Research Study 83 (London: HMSO).

Rojek, C., Peacock, G. & Collins, S. (1988) *Social Work and Received Ideas* (London: Routledge).

Roll, J. (1990) *Young People: Growing Up in the Welfare State* (London: Family Policy Studies Centre).

Rose, E. A. (1982) *Housing Needs and the Elderly* (Aldershot: Gower).

Sainsbury, E. *et al.* (1982) *Social Work in Focus: clients and social workers' perceptions in long-term social work* (London: Routledge & Kegan Paul).

Sampford, C. J. G. & Galligan, D. J. (eds) (1986) *Law, Rights and the Welfare State* (London: Croom Helm).

Satyamurti, C. (1981) *Occupational Survival: the case of the local authority social worker* (Oxford: Blackwell).

Scottish Development Department (1980) *Housing (Homeless Persons) Act 1977, Code of Guidance – Scotland* (Edinburgh: Scottish Development Department).

Scottish Law Commission (1980) *Report on Occupancy Rights in the Matrimonial Home and Domestic Violence*, session 1979–80, HCP 676 (London: HMSO).

Sedley, S. (Chair) (1987) *Whose Child? Report of the Public Inquiry Into the Death of Tyra Henry* (London Borough of Lambeth).

Seebohm, F. (Chair) (1968) *Report of the Committee on Local Authority and Allied Personal Social Services*, Cmnd.3703 (London: HMSO).

Sharpe, C. (1991) *Problems Assured* (London: SHAC).

Sharpe, S. (1987) *Falling For Love: Teenage Mothers Talk* (London: Virago).

Short, J. R. (1982) *Housing in Britain: the post-war experience* (London: Methuen).

Simpson, A. (1982) *Stacking the Decks: A Study of Race, Inequality and Council Housing* (Nottingham: Community Relations Council).

Sinclair, I & Walker, D. (1985) 'Task-centred casework in two intake teams' in E. M. Golding *et al.*, *Problems, Tasks and Outcomes* (London: Allen & Unwin).

Smith, K. (1986) *I'm Not Complaining: the housing conditions of elderly private tenants* (London: SHAC).

Smith, L. J. F. (1989) *Domestic Violence: an overview of the literature*, Home Office Research Study 107 (London: HMSO).

Smith, N. J. (1966) 'Social problems of new housing estates' in *Case Conference*, vol. 13, no. 3, pp. 101–5.

Smith, S. J. (1989) *Housing and Health: a review and research agenda* (Glasgow: Centre for Housing Research, University of Glasgow).

Social Security Advisory Committee (1986) *Proposals for Regulations to Provide a New Scheme of Supplementary Benefit Exceptionally Severe Weather Payment*, Cm.18 (London: HMSO).

Social Security Policy Inspectorate (1986) *Enquiry Into Mortgage Interest* (London: DHSS).

Social Services Inspectorate (1985) *Assessment Procedures for Elderly People Referred for Local Authority Residential Care* (London: DHSS).

Social Services Inspectorate London Region (1989A) *Notes of a Study Day on Family Homelessness* (London: SSI London Region).

Social Services Inspectorate London Region (1989B) *Report of a Study Day on Family Homelessness, 1987* (London: Department of Health).

Sorensen, M. (1986) *Working on Self-Respect* (London: Peter Bedford Trust).

Southwark Area Review Committee (1989) *The Doreen Aston Report* (London: Lewisham Social Services Dept).

Spicker, P. (1986) 'Confessions of a lettings officer' in *Community Care*, 6 November, pp. 18–19.

Spicker, P. (1987) 'Concepts of need in housing allocation' in *Policy and Politics*, vol. 15, no. 1, pp. 17–27.

Stein, M. & Carey, K. (1986) *Leaving Cure* (Oxford: Blackwell).

Stevenson, O. & Parsloe, P. (1978) *Social Service Teams: The Practitioner's View* (London: HMSO).

Stewart, J. & Stewart, G. (eds) (1982) *Social Work and Homelessness* (Lancaster: Lancaster University, Department of Social Administration).

Stewart, G. & Stewart, J. (1986A) *Boundary Changes: social work and social security*, Poverty Pamphlet 70 (London: Child Poverty Action Group & British Association of Social Workers).

Stewart, G., Lee, R. & Stewart, J. (1986B) 'The right approach to social security: the case of the board and lodging regulations' in *Journal of Law and Society* vol. 13 no. 3, pp. 371–99.

Stewart, G. & Tutt, N. (1987) *Children in Custody* (Aldershot: Avebury).

Stewart, G. & Stewart, J. (1988) 'Targeting youth, or how the state obstructs young people's independence' in *Youth and Policy*, no. 25, pp. 19–24.

Stewart, G., Stewart, J., Peelo, M. & Prior, A. (1989) *Surviving Poverty: probation work and benefits policy* (Wakefield: Association of Chief Officers of Probation).

Stewart, G., Stewart, J., Peelo, M. & Prior, A. (1990) 'Squeezing the Social Fund: aggravation and advocacy' in *Probation Journal*, vol. 37, no. 3, pp. 131–4.

Stewart, G. & Stewart, J. (1991) *Relieving Poverty? Use of the Social Fund by Social Work Clients and Other Agencies* (London: Association of Metropolitan Authorities).

Stewart, G. & Stewart, J. (1992A) 'Social work with homeless families', *British Journal of Social Work*, vol. 22, no. 3, pp. 271–89.

Stewart, G. & Stewart, J. (1992B) 'The politics of the Social Fund', forthcoming in *Local Government Studies*.

Struyk, R. T. (1987) 'The economic behaviour of elderly people in housing markets' in *Housing Studies*, vol. 2, no. 4, pp. 221–36.

Sullivan, O. (1986) 'Housing movements of the divorced and separated' in *Housing Studies*, vol. 1, no. 1, January, pp. 35–48.

Swain, K. (1986) 'Probation attitudes to battered women: apathy, error and avoidance?' in *Probation Journal*, vol. 33, no. 4, December, pp. 132–4.

Symon, P. (ed.) (1990) *Housing and Divorce* (Glasgow: Centre for Housing Research, University of Glasgow).

Taylor, H. (1987) *Growing Old Together: elderly owner-occupiers and their housing* (London: Centre for Policy on Ageing).

Thoburn, J. (1980) *Captive Clients: social work with families of children home on trial* (London: Routledge).

Thomas, A. & Niner, P. (1989) *Living in Temporary Accommodation: A Survey of Homeless People* (London: HMSO).

Timaeus, I. (1990) 'The fall in the number of children in care: a demographic analysis' in *Journal of Social Policy*, vol. 19 no. 3, pp. 375–96.

Tinker, A. (1984) *Staying at Home: helping elderly people* (London: HMSO).

Todd, J. E. (1986) *Recent Private Lettings 1982–84* (London: HMSO).

Treasury (1988) *The Government's Expenditure Plans 1988–89 to 1990–91*, Cm. 288 (London: HMSO).

Treasury (1989) *The Government's Expenditure Plans 1989–90 to 1991–92*, Cm. 609 (London: HMSO).

Tuckley, W. (1985) *Relationship Breakdown and Local Authority Tenancies: a GLC survey of London housing authorities' policies toward relationship breakdown among tenants in local authority housing* (London: Greater London Council).

Tyler, M. (1978) *Advisory and Counselling Services For Young People*, DHSS Research Report no. 1 (London: HMSO).

Underwood, S. *et al.* (1986) *Who Lives In Housing Co-operatives: The Report of a National Survey of Housing Co-operatives and their Tenant Members* (London: National Federation of Housing Associations).

Venn, S. (1985) *Singled Out: Local Authority Housing Policies for Single People* (London: CHAR Campaign for Single Homeless People).

Violence Against Children Study Group (1990) *Taking Child Abuse Seriously* (London: Unwin Hyman).

Walker, A. (1985) *The Care Gap: how can local authorities meet the needs of the elderly?* (London: Local Government Information Unit).

Walker, H. (1991) 'Family centres' in P. Carter, T. Jeffs & M. Smith (eds) *Social Work and Social Welfare Yearbook 3* (Milton Keynes: Open University Press).

Wandsworth Area Child Protection Committee (1990) *The Report of the Stephanie Fox Practice Review* (London: Wandsworth Social Services Dept).

Ware, V. (1988) *Women's Safety on Housing Estates* (London: Women's Design Service).

Weller, M., Tobiansky, R. I., Hollander, D. & Ibrahimi, S. (1989) 'Psychosis and destitution at Christmas 1985–88' in *The Lancet*, 23–30 December, pp. 1509–11.

Welsh Women's Aid (1986) *The Answer is Maybe . . . and that's final!* (Cardiff: Welsh Women's Aid).

Wertheimer, A. (1988) *Housing Consortia for Community Care* (London: National Federation of Housing Associations/NCVO).

Wertheimer, A. (1989) *Housing: the Foundation of Community Care*, 2nd edition (London: National Federation of Housing Associations/Mind).

Wheeler, R. (1986) 'Housing policy and elderly people' in C. Phillipson & A. Walker (eds) *Ageing and Social Policy* (Aldershot: Gower).

White, M. (ed.) (1987) *The Social World of the Young Unemployed* (London: Policy Studies Institute).

Whitman, B. Y., Accardo, P., Boyert, M. & Kendagor, R. (1990, 'Homelessness and cognitive performance in children: a possible link' in *Social Work*, vol. 35, no. 6, pp. 516–19.

Whynes, D. K. (1990) 'Reported health problems and the socio-economic characteristics of the single homeless' in *British Journal of Social Work*, vol. 20, no. 4, pp. 355–71.

Wicks, M. (1978) *Old and Cold: hypothermia and social policy* (London: Heinemann).

Wiggans, A. (1982) *Away From the Bright Lights: Youth Work and Homelessness* (Leicester: National Association of Youth Clubs).

Wilkes, R. (1981) *Social Work with Undervalued Groups* (London: Tavistock).

Wilkinson, A. (1983) 'Children who come into care in Tower Hamlets' in *Social Services Research*, no. 1, pp. 63–107.

Williams, S. & Allen, I. (1989) *Health Care for Single Homeless People* (London: Policy Studies Institute).

Wilson, H. & Herbert, G. W. (1978) *Parents and Children in the Inner City* (London: Routledge).

Wolinski, A. (1984) *Osmondthorpe: A Study of Community Work on an Inter-War Council Estate* (Ilford: Dr.Barnardo's).

Woodward, R. (1991) 'Mobilising opposition: the campaign against Housing Action Trusts in Tower Hamlets' in *Housing Studies*, vol. 6 no. 1, pp.44–56.

York, A. S. (1976) 'Voluntary associations in a "difficult" housing estate' in *Community Development Journal*, vol. 11, no. 2, pp. 126–33.

Index